SEEKING A
familiar
FACE

The Transformational Journey
of Connecting with God

BY MAY PATTERSON

Seeking a Familiar Face: The Transforming Journey of Connecting with God

© 2017 by May Patterson. All rights reserved. Published by Exploration Press.

Author Website and Blog: maypatterson.com
Cover & Interior Design: Andrea Wilhelm
Cover Image: Cococinema/Shutterstock

Contents

1

SEEKING A FAMILIAR FACE:
Locking Hearts with God 7

2

JOSIAH:
Seeking Changes Everything 19

3

MOSES:
Seeking Lifts Our Hearts 31

4

THE THIEF:
Seeking Invites Grace 47

5

MARY OF BETHANY:
Seeking Fills Us with God's Love 61

6

ZACCHAEUS:
Seeking Frees Us from Bondage 75

7

DAVID:
Seeking Enhances Our Worship 87

8

ELIJAH:
Seeking Strengthens Our Prayer Life 103

9

RUTH:
Seeking Helps Us Love Others Well 119

10

HANNAH:
Seeking Leads to Surrender 135

11

BARNABAS:
Seeking Helps Us Discover Our Gifts 149

12

WHEN SEEKING ENDS:
Seeing God Face to Face 165

Acknowledgements 171
Notes 174

To fall in love with God is the greatest romance; to seek Him the greatest adventure; to find Him, the greatest human achievement.

ST. AUGUSTINE

CHAPTER 1

Seeking a Familiar Face:

Locking Hearts with God

Keep on asking, and you will receive what you ask for.
Keep on seeking, and you will find. Keep on knocking,
and the door will be opened to you.

MATTHEW 7:7 NLT

Venice, Italy, is a city like no other. I discovered that the day
I stepped off a water-taxi and into its spaghetti-like snarl of
nameless, narrow streets. A medieval town with no cars (or cabs)
is very hard to navigate on foot with luggage in tow. I was alone
and exhausted, having traveled all night to meet my daughter,
Caroline, who was studying abroad. But instead of meeting her, I
encountered a thousand strangers in St. Mark's Square.

I had no idea how to get to my hotel. I asked the man at the
water-taxi stand, but he didn't know where it was. I asked a
heavy-set lady from Texas, and she said, "Honey, I'm just as lost
as you are." I asked some locals at a coffee shop for help, but no

one seemed to know (or care enough to show me) where the Best Western was. How hard could it be to find on an island?

Pretty hard, actually.

Venice has ten Best Western hotels—an obscure, but critical fact that I was unaware of. And I didn't know exactly which one I was trying to find. Many of the streets are poorly marked, if marked at all, so the address I had in my pocket wasn't very helpful. I couldn't pull up the information or call the hotel, because earlier I had decided that an international cellular plan was too expensive. Big mistake.

Up and over the arched bridges I went, pulling my heavy black bag behind me, searching for the obscure street on a confusing Italian map. The sun began to set, bathing the ancient buildings in a pale golden light. It was beautiful, but as I shivered in the cold, Venice quickly began to lose its appeal. Feeling weary and utterly frustrated, I rifled through my bag for my hat and gloves. Oh, how I longed for a familiar face! A tear trickled down my cheek as I realized how far from home I was and how lost I felt. I didn't know what to do next, so I sat on a bench and scanned the crowd. So many people and yet, I didn't know a single one.

Finally, something caught my eye—a gray coat with a ruffled hem that I thought I'd seen before. I stood on top of the wooden bench to get a better look, searching again for that glimpse of the familiar. Finally, my gaze zeroed in on a single face within the sea of faces.

Even from thirty yards away, I recognized her. A sudden memory of her face as a little child looking up at me flashed through my mind. I hadn't seen my nineteen-year-old daughter in a long time, but I knew every detail of her face and the earnest expression in her dark brown eyes. In that moment, she looked more beautiful than ever. A sense of home and belonging was captured in one beloved face. Caroline was out searching for me.

I remember simply staring at her for a second, my eyes and heart connecting before I could even speak or move. We had never been apart for so long, and now, just when I felt so alone and lost, there she was! Finding a familiar face in a foreign place flooded my heart with delight and relief. Five thousand miles away from home, I found someone who knew me, but more importantly, I found someone who *loved* me.

Only those who have been lost know the joy of being found. What a sense of connection! I've never been so glad to find someone. I jumped up and down on the bench, dancing with joy and yelling her name. When she ran over, I wrapped her in a desperate hug, picked her up, and spun her in a circle. It was glorious!

SEEKING AND FINDING

This experience of longing and searching, finding and connecting is the same glorious feeling we can have when we seek God and find Him. From far away, we know Him. The closer we get, the greater our joy becomes. When His heart connects with ours, we experience a wonderful dance of delight, love, and relief. His soul touches ours—and it is beautiful. Powerful. Life changing.

I know about this connection with God, only because I have felt it. At one time, I didn't know the experience of locking hearts with Him, deeply connecting, and actually *feeling* His presence was possible. One of the greatest blessings of being God's child is that we can have this sense of belonging, joy, and connection every day by seeking and finding Him.

We are all seekers in one way or another. Consider how children naturally play hide-and-seek. They love the process of seeking for someone, followed by the thrill of finding them. Adults love it too. That's why the Discovery Channel and geocaching are so popular. The desire to seek and find drove those who explored the Wild West. It sent others to space. Sometimes, it sends me to the mall! We all participate in life's hide-and-seek in some way.

I saw this concept come to life once on a rainy summer afternoon. We were stuck indoors due to the weather, so my bored little children began playing hide-and-seek. Searching and finding brought squeals of delight along with intense intrigue. Little feet scampered excitedly down the hall to search for one another and for new hiding places. To my surprise, my son Will actually found a place that none of us knew existed: an open space behind the shelves of our deep TV cabinet. Will crawled underneath the cabinet and up into this space to hide. It was the greatest hiding place *ever*.

The other children were determined to find his secret hiding place. The rainy hours went by quickly as they searched. Finally, Will was caught sneaking out of the cabinet and the secret was out. The kids giggled with delight; seeking and finding made their day.

The question is, do we play hide-and-seek with God? Is God hiding or lost? Is this just some cosmic game God wants us to play? Hardly. God is always with us, yet we can ignore Him pretty easily and go our own way. We can quickly lose awareness that He is there, disregard His direction, and miss the benefits and joys of His promises. Seeking after God keeps our lives connected to His.

GOD ASKS US TO SEEK

The Bible is full of stories about people who sought to understand, know, and experience God in different ways. Each one had difficulties. Some were afraid. Others were in desperate need. These seekers turned to God in their own unique way and found Him. We can learn from their experiences.

Josiah set his heart to seek after a God he knew very little about. Frustrated Moses stepped out of the pit of despair by witnessing God's glory. A shirtless David danced joyfully with his people in a once-in-a-lifetime worship experience. Hannah went to God's house in order to build her own. Elijah's prayer received a lightening-bolt answer. The dying thief on the cross desperately reached out and found life. They all went looking for God and each one found a unique reward.

All of these seekers set their hearts on a journey beyond what they could see, to gain something that no one could take away. Their ordinary lives were transformed by encountering the extraordinary God. We have the same opportunity. We have different problems and different approaches, but we share the same God. He wants to be found and to connect with us. In fact, He is searching for you and me right now. God uses our times of connection with Him to strengthen our souls, shape our minds, and transform our hearts. Seeking God is worth every moment we spend doing it.

Although this opportunity to know God more fully exists for everyone, many Christians feel distant from Him. Some have never really made a connection. Others have neglected it. Unfortunately, we often fail to seek God until a crisis comes along. But when we make the *investment* of searching for God, finding Him will fill our lives with a sense of wonder and joy. When we connect with Him over and over, His face begins to feel familiar, like home.

As we begin our journey through this book together, it's important to know why God asks us to seek Him (Isa. 55:6-7).

It's pretty simple, really: *the reason we seek the Lord is to know Him more fully.*

That used to be kind of vague to me. But I've learned that knowing God is not the same as knowing *about* God. Anyone can study about Him, but we can come to know God only by experiencing Him in prayer and worship and while loving and serving others. To experience God, we must make ourselves available for an ongoing relationship. We know the Lord when we lock hearts. We understand Him better as we study His Word. We perceive His thoughts and leading by being filled with His Spirit. We can feel His presence with us and in us. This kind of intimacy takes time—actually a lifetime. Even after seeking God every day for the rest of our lives, we will have only just begun to truly know Him. The Bible says the Lord is beyond tracing out (Rom. 11:33). I love that. With God, there is always something more to discover. Knowing this adds vibrancy and wonder to every seeker's life.

A. W. Tozer wrote, "God wills that we would push into His presence and live our whole life there."[1] But how do we do that, exactly? We can learn a lot by looking at the way others have done it. The chapters in this book focus on the stories of real-life people in the Bible who sought God in different ways. Chapters include a fictionalized narrative about what *might* have caused each one to seek God, how they must have felt, and what he or she found.

Since we all approach God uniquely, I've added questions at the end of each chapter that will help you explore ways to seek God for yourself. You are probably already doing some things that can draw you near to God, but I want to take you further. These Seek and Find questions will help you seek God in new ways and also reinforce the ways you are already seeking Him.

Many of the questions can also be used to inspire discussion with others who are seeking. Sharing your journey of seeking and finding God with others is a powerful experience. Consider using the section at the end of each chapter in a small group or Bible study. Seeking with a group will enrich your journey, deepen your joy, and bring you closer to others.

PRACTICAL STEPS

While there is no one right way to seek God, there are some common practices that can help:

A Commitment. First Chronicles 22:19 says, "Now devote your heart and soul to seeking the Lord. . ." I am not always good at devoting myself to something. New Year's resolutions usually end by February. My dieting is on and off. And oh, how easily I can skip going to the gym! But seeking God is not like that. We can find a lot of help with the commitment part if we pray for God to help us seek Him. As you read through this book, try to do something each day to reach out to God. It can be something simple like a special prayer, meditating on a verse, or doing something for someone else. The key is to do at least *one thing per day* to seek God until you can easily recognize His face. Doing this will help you know Him better and open the door to numerous blessings (Heb. 11:6).

A Place. Another practical step is to have a designated "seeking place" (or several). One of my seeking places is outdoors, where I pray, think, and reach out to God while I walk. Even while I'm in motion, my heart can be still and fixed on God. Some mornings I seek the Lord in the swing on my screened porch. The birds sing, as if to cheer me on. After a while, I find His familiar face and feel the connection once again.

That's the thing about seeking Him—it's really not that hard. It just takes intention, awareness, and a little time each day.

A Plan. Mark Batterson writes, "One of the reasons that many people don't feel an intimacy with God is because they don't have a daily rhythm with God; they have a *weekly* rhythm. Would that work with your spouse or your kids? It doesn't work in God's family either."[2] This means we have to plan to seek God or it may not happen. There are a lot of different ways to do this, but here are a few ideas:

Use the questions in the Seek and Find sections of this book as a guide. There are journaling ideas, meditations, and questions designed to enrich your seeking experience.

- Before you go to church, dedicate the worship service to seeking and finding God. You might pray, "I'm looking for you today, God. Reveal yourself to me in a special way while I worship. Fill me with awe in your presence." This will help you consciously seek God's face during the service, and you will probably get more out it.

- Dedicate your good works as part of seeking God. Do each thing for His glory. Use your good works as a canvas upon which to paint the beauty and value of God. Working for and with God helps us know Him more fully and it helps us discover and develop our gifts.

- Pray all day, without ceasing. Keep it conversational, as if God is right next to you. This involves Him in all aspects of your life—not just in the "religious" parts.

- Practice finding your story in each of the character stories in this book. Even though your circumstances may be different, you still experience similar emotions and problems. Study how they sought after God and how He responded—this will give you insight into how He may respond to you.

- Love others as a way of drawing near to God's heart. Tell the Lord you are showing love to His children because you love Him.

- Meditate. Consider how connecting with God feels physically, emotionally, and spiritually. Meditate on the power and peace that God gives you as seek Him each day.

- Vary what you do each day to seek God. Look for new ways to find Him. Each chapter in this book will give you a different perspective on seeking, along with practical ideas.

- Journal about what you learn as you are seeking, as if documenting a journey. A journal is useful to any traveler—whether you are a writer or not. If you have an experience of finding God, make sure you write it down and date it. Many people resist journaling. I sure did! I still don't journal every day, but I try to document every time God teaches me something. Every time I feel lost or distant and find Him, I write about it. Journaling keeps new discoveries and lessons alive. I certainly don't want to repeat some lessons more than once! Journaling helps me remember.

- Pray on paper. Tell the Lord what is weighing on your heart. Writing my prayers often helps me look for God in a roundabout way, kind of like I did with Caroline in Venice. And when I look back at my journals, I notice thoughts and words that I know didn't really come from me. It's amazing to witness how God responds to the seeking heart.

When we seek God faithfully, we find Him. And then, we seek Him some more. Seeking and finding the Lord is the ultimate life adventure. We have no idea where we will go or what we will find. Our journey becomes a series of awe-inspiring encounters. Soon, we start living in amazement and wonder at all the blessings of knowing Him better. We find things that surprise and delight us. We tap into the power to live differently. And on hard days when we feel like we are lost and alone in a foreign place, we catch a glimpse of a familiar face and find a loving God who has been out looking for us all along.

Seek and Find

1. Seeking God is mentioned more than fifty times in the Bible. That means it's important to do. But for some, it's more of an occasional thing, and consequently, their souls suffer. God asks us to *practice* seeking and finding Him repeatedly because this keeps our heart connected to His. As you begin to think about what seeking God means to you, find five references to seeking in the Bible. List the rewards and benefits that are promised. If you're reading this book with a small group, share what you have found in your Scripture search.

2. Contemplate my story of seeking and finding in Venice. Have you ever felt lost like that? Have you ever found and locked hearts with God, just when you felt like you needed Him the most? Journal your answers or share them with your group.

3. What might stand in the way of your seeking? Are you facing specific problems that seem to distance you from God? Write or share about your personal obstacles.

4. Describe your "seeking place." If you don't have one, consider designating a place in your home and furnishing it with a Bible, pen, paper, index cards, and so on.

5. Write out a seeking plan for this week. Ideas: dedicate a worship time to seeking God; decide what to do in daily quiet time that might help you feel God's presence; write a specific prayer or slogan to reflect on throughout the week. If you're meeting with a group, share next time what you did and what it taught you about seeking and finding God.

CHAPTER 2

Josiah

Seeking Changes Everything

With God, it isn't who you were that matters;
it's who you are becoming.

LIZ CURTIS HIGGS

Ever notice the roaming feature on your cell phone? Our phones
search and search until they find a signal. And wow, when a
smartphone connects, isn't it powerful? It's called "smart" for a
reason. I can talk to someone in a mud-thatched hut in Kenya as I
walk down a Florida beach. I can talk to someone standing in an
Alabama cotton field while I'm on the chairlift in Colorado (that
actually happened). I can shop at Nordstrom while I'm in bed at
midnight. (That can be dangerous.)

But a smartphone does even more than that: it's a directional
device, a calculator, a tape recorder, a flashlight, and a camera.
Years ago, separate devices were required for all of those
functions. Now one little phone performs more functions than most
of us know how to use, and we rely on it for everything. But until

we had a smartphone, we didn't know how much we needed it.

It's the same with the practice of seeking God. Once we realize how powerful and helpful it is, we will begin to rely on it heavily. Soon, we will wonder how we could possibly live our lives without seeking the Lord every day. But like the cell phone, we have to seek to connect. It may require some roaming time. But when we find Him, we are changed.

Consider the dramatic effect that seeking God had on the life of King Josiah and the world around him.

Josiah Seeks

His scream was excruciating—sometimes I can still hear it. The mosaic tiles were smeared with blood. Terror infused the air. Daggers littered the floor. I was only eight years old when I found my father, King Amon, lying face down in a crimson pool of blood. He had been murdered. His golden crown lay in his outstretched hand, as if he was extending his legacy to me. From that day on, I would wear his bloodstained crown, haunted by the fear of the same grisly destiny.

The next few years were spent just trying to survive the dark, savage chaos that followed. Babies were sacrificed to appease the gods. Pagan sexual rituals were practiced at the temple to boost the harvest. Murder was so commonplace that it often went unpunished. I soon realized that even my own family couldn't be trusted—each one wanted my crown. Their lust for power rendered them incapable of love.

Violence was all I knew. Like a rotten apple fallen from a rotten tree, I would have been just like my father, but seeing his dreadful death drove me in a different direction. One day an advisor told me the story of King David, my ancestor, who was once a shepherd but became a great king. It was then that I realized, changing my destiny was possible.

So, at the age of sixteen, I adopted King David as my role model. I dedicated my heart to seeking David's God—and I found Him to be near. Since the Law of Moses had been lost before I was born, I set out to seek after a God I really didn't know much about. I questioned palace historians, prophets, and Levites, trying to learn all I could about God. I started a morning ritual of prayer and meditation. Soon, I began to sense that God was listening. Seeking God every day helped me come to know His greatness. Spending time with God changed me, and eventually these changes rippled out to my entire nation.

But it happened slowly. During my first four years of seeking God, nothing really changed in Jerusalem. Daily debauchery. Rampant idolatry. Common cruelty. But as God changed me inwardly, I became increasingly aware of the evil within my kingdom and I resolved to stand against it. God showed me how to live differently, yet for a while, it seemed like the world around me stayed the same—or got even worse.

Finally, God revealed to me that idolatry was the root cause of my people's problems. So, at twenty years old, I began a lifelong quest to tear down idols, smash sacred stones, and desecrate pagan altars. This wasn't popular. My overly superstitious people lived in constant fear of the gods. But God's greatness inspired me to persevere, and soon I became known as "Josiah, the Great Reformer." It took me years to dislodge the painful thorn of idolatry from the heart of our nation, but as I did, healing began.

When I was twenty-six, I renovated the damaged temple of God. One day, the Law of Moses was found, tucked away in a storeroom. When I heard its words, I wept and tore my robes, realizing that—as far as we had come—we were still living in rebellion against God. I read the words to the people, and we made a covenant to end idolatry, child sacrifice, and pagan rituals. Repentance breathed spiritual life back into our nation, bringing peace, prosperity, and freedom.

I am the son of Judah's worst king, but seeking God helped me change my destiny. In the presence of His greatness, I became great. Just like King David before me, I earned the praise of God. Later it would be said of me, "Neither before nor after Josiah was there a king like him who turned to the Lord like he did—with all his heart and with all his soul and with all his strength . . ." (2 Ki. 23:25).

Josiah saved himself and an entire generation from disaster. He brought peace and prosperity to a nation choking on idolatry and violence. And the blessings of Josiah's seeking ripple on; thousands of years later *we* are blessed by his story too. God has placed an innate desire within each of us to seek after Him so that we will discover His greatness. Josiah found more than he ever expected with God. We are guaranteed to find the same kind of "more" too, for He rewards those who diligently seek Him (Heb. 11:6).

THE REWARDS OF SEEKING

Consider the life-changing blessings Josiah found by seeking and finding the Lord, and ponder how they can be yours as well.

Seeking God enables self-awareness. In God's light we can see truth about our lives, just like Josiah did. An accurate view of ourselves enables us to address our weaknesses, stop destructive behaviors, and change the course of our lives.

Seeking changes our personal destiny. It loosens us from

the grip of the past and from generational sin. God's greatness
rubs off on us. His glory transforms our lives, allowing us to
rise above any deficits in our rearing to fully become who God
designed us to be.

Seeking God affects other people. The blessings of Josiah's
seeking rippled out to save his entire generation. Josiah's powerful
story has blessed many people throughout the ages, including
us today. Like Josiah, our seeking after God will affect family,
friends, and future generations too. Consider who might be
affected by your seeking the Lord. How might your quest bless
other people in your life?

Josiah sought after God with "all of his heart" (2 Ki. 23:25). I
think that means he searched for God often. Daily. Habitually. On
busy days that can be difficult to do. We can easily get sidetracked
with distractions. We may be overwhelmed with pain or
responsibility. Maybe God gave us Josiah's story to encourage us
to seek Him *right now*. We can't see our entire story yet, but if we
could ask Josiah, he would probably say, "Go ahead, roam. Seek
to make the connection every day. It will change everything."

A lot of other people in the Bible sought a connection with
God too. For example, Genesis 5:24 tells us, "Enoch walked
faithfully with God . . ." The Hebrew translation means "rubbed
shoulders with God." I like that mental picture; spending time
with God enables us to walk beside Him, shoulder to shoulder,
bringing us into close proximity to His heart. And when we think
we've moved as close to God as we possibly can, there is always
room to move even closer.

MY JOURNEY
When I started my own journey of seeking God, I soon discovered

that He was much different than I expected—and so was I.

I remember feeling trapped—like a fifty-pound weight was permanently attached to my shoulders. Life just wasn't as fulfilling as I had always dreamed it would be. Josiah probably felt that way—laden with responsibilities, overwhelmed but empty, maybe a bit . . . caged. These same feelings drove me to start my own journey of seeking God.

I had a two-year-old, and then, have mercy, twin boys! I often daydreamed about running away and living with friends on the beach. Permanently. I struggled to bear the responsibility of three young lives because I was pretty focused on my own. My goal of a fun life evaporated under the weight of dirty diapers and forced insomnia. I was barely surviving. I loved my family too much to leave, so I stayed and was miserable—lucky them.

This crisis finally drove me to reach out to God, because obviously I had missed something with Him—the *joy* of connection. Although I had grown up in church, I couldn't describe God's personality because I didn't know Him very well. So like Josiah, I set out on my own journey of seeking a God I didn't really know. I started spending small amounts of time with God each day—reading, praying, listening, doing little things to reach out. I listened to a sermon series entitled "Who is God?" on my Walkman (kinda makes me feel old). As I pursued Him, I quickly learned that seeking God is not a random side trip; it is a lifelong journey, an active search for something more that offers magnificent rewards. This seeking was new for me, and it gave me a new sense of purpose.

To my surprise, the more I discovered about God, the more I discovered about myself. For instance, I grew up thinking my life had no particular destiny. I just wanted to be happy, so I focused on me. I believed God helped me sometimes, but He

wasn't overly involved. As I studied God's personality, I learned
that God was sovereign over everything. That meant me . . .
and every detail of my entire life. Maybe having three babies in
two years was not a random act of nature (or fertility drugs). I
realized God had planned it, so I would seek and find Him. My
life had a detailed design for a reason—so that I would know
God more fully and rub shoulders with Him like Enoch and
Josiah did.

God's sovereignty means that He reigns over my
circumstances, good or bad. I learned that He uses the hard
things, the mundane things, and the unfair things—in other
words, everything—for our good. Feeling trapped, unfulfilled,
and over-burdened was actually a blessing, because it drove
me to my knees and closer to God's heart. That's where the
miracle of transformation occurs: near the heart of God. God is
remarkably personal with each of us—much more than I ever
thought.

This growing intimacy helped me overcome feeling helpless,
like a pinball being knocked around from one hard place to the
next. Playing the pitiful martyr-with-three-babies role allowed
me to blame circumstances, other people, and even God for my
unhappiness. But if God was sovereign, I had to accept His plan
and stop blaming and complaining. I am not the "poor wayfaring
stranger traveling through this world of woe," like the old
depressing song says. I am running a race He has designed just
for me!

This was a real game changer. Learning this dried up some
of my teary self-pity and replaced it with a smile of gratitude—
especially for my children. Even though complaining comes
pretty naturally to me (I'm working on that), I have learned to
see it as a sin from which I need to turn away.

My discoveries taught me that seeking God is an *adventure*. The more I discovered, the more eager I was to see what else I might find. This sense of wonder and awe allowed me to press back against my demanding life instead of collapsing beneath its weight. As the knowledge of God began to grow brighter in my heart and I actually experienced His presence, my life seemed a little easier and much more interesting.

These were the first discoveries of my seeking journey, but not the last. Like Josiah, my changed thinking changed everything else, not only for me, but for my family too. (My husband, Mike, is especially grateful!) Now, seemingly overnight, my children are grown. Thankfully, seeking God rescued me from the pit of ingratitude before I totally ruined their childhood and missed some precious moments. Being a mother is my God-given privilege. Realizing this gave me the strength to handle the stress of all those babies at once. And God gave me a deep love for each one of them.

Seeking God has a ripple effect from here to eternity, touching individuals, lives, and circumstances more than we may ever know.

REACH OUT AND TOUCH ME

In 1979, AT&T ads used the award-winning slogan, "Reach out and touch someone." Did they plagiarize it from Acts 17? I'll let you decide. "From one man he made all the people of the world. Now they live all over the earth. He decided exactly when they should live. And he decided exactly where they should live. God did this so that people would seek him. And perhaps they would reach out for him and find him. They would find him even though he is not far from any of us" (Acts 17:26-27 NIRV).

"Reach out and touch me," God says. Our exact times and places are designed to connect us to Him. Think of where you are right now. Could God be using your circumstances to connect with you on a deeper level? Maybe God is reaching out to you through this book (I hope so) to draw you even nearer.

Lelia Morris, writer of the old hymn "Nearer Still Nearer," understood the concept of seeking as a journey. She described its destination beautifully:

> *Nearer still nearer, while life shall last,*
> *till safe in glory my anchor is cast;*
> *through endless ages, ever to be*
> *nearer, my Savior, still nearer to the thee .*

In James 4:8, God says, "Come near to me, and I will come near to you" (my paraphrase). In other words, God wants to connect. And our souls hunger for this nearness. I starved my poor soul for way too long. Connecting with God has transformed my life and helped me grow in ways I never could have imagined, taking me nearer to His heart.

God plans the journey of each of His beloved children—Josiah's, yours, and mine. Josiah and the other seekers in this book are examples of how seeking can bless us and those around us. Set some time aside every day just for God; examine the different aspects of His personality—you might just discover some things about yourself. The time for seeking is our lifetime—and it will change everything.

Seek and Find

1. Read 2 Kings 23-24. As you review the timeline of Josiah's seeking journey (below), consider where you are in your own journey and where you'd like to go. If you're in a small group, answer the questions together:

Age 16:

Begins to seek the Lord as a practice.
In what ways have you done this?

Ages 16-20:

No outward change.
Can you relate? Does it seem like nothing is changing for you right now? During this time, changes happened inwardly to Josiah as he began to notice the sin around him. He learned to live differently than anyone he may have ever known. In what ways are you learning—or do you want to learn—to live differently?

Age 20:

Begins to pursue his life calling of reformation.
He removed idols from Judah and destroyed ritual sites intended for child sacrifice. Are you beginning to pursue your personal ministry or calling? How?

Age 26:

Develops his calling further by repairing the temple and restoring worship there (including reinstating the Passover).
How are you developing your talents and working out your calling?

Age 26:

Saves his entire generation from destruction.
Who might your seeking affect?

Ages 26-39:

*Continues to remove idols from Judah and even removes them
from neighboring countries.*
Name some ways in which you might continue seeking God and
live out your calling, like Josiah did.

2. If God rewarded Josiah for seeking after Him, then He will
also reward you. Looking at Josiah's timeline, what specific
things did Josiah gain from seeking the Lord repeatedly? What
have you gained from seeking? What would you like to gain as
you go forward?

CHAPTER 3

Moses

Seeking Lifts Our Hearts

The best we can hope for in this life is a knothole peek at the shining realities ahead. Yet a glimpse is enough. It's enough to convince our hearts that whatever sufferings and sorrows currently assail us aren't worthy of comparison to that which waits over the horizon.

JONI EARECKSON TADA

Have you ever stood at the rim of the Grand Canyon? Or seen the waves crash on a rocky shore? What about that tropical sunset, where you stood awestruck, watching a ball of orange slowly melt into a cobalt sea? In these moments our hearts cannot help but praise. These "glory moments" temporarily transcend our problems and heartaches. Our hearts are lifted and we come away thankful. Stronger. Lighter than before.

We love the beauty of creation because it points us to the Creator. It promises us that He must be even more majestic and beautiful than anything we can see. We all crave beauty and greatness. We all seek a hero to worship. Creation tells us that God is great and glorious. His glory fulfills our need for a true hero. It inspires us to go on and do great things.

Moses was called by God to persevere as he led the Israelites through the wilderness to the Promised Land. When they rebelled against God by worshipping the golden calf, Moses was discouraged. From the depths of despair, he asked an unusual question: to see God's glory. God agreed. That one glimpse of God's glory lifted Moses's heart and gave him the strength to keep moving forward. And seeking God's glory can do the same thing for us.

Moses Seeks

I am really fed up. Worn out. Done. I sigh as a blast of hot wind whips across my face. On Mt. Sinai, there are no sprigs of grass, no signs of water, nothing but rocks and sand as far as I can see. The desert has been my home for years; its harsh conditions don't bother me. But the Israelites complain about the heat and desolation of this place *every single day*.

I am not accustomed to trying to meet the needs of so many. Bearing the weight of an entire nation on my shoulders is just too heavy. Now God has called me back up the mountain and, truthfully, I'm glad to get away. The Israelites are stubborn; I can't seem to lead them very well, even though I've tried.

After all the Lord has done for us, their worship of the golden calf was the last straw. No matter how many miracles they see, the Israelites continually turn away from God. My teaching has been pretty ineffective. I feel as dry inside as the parched ground beneath my feet. In righteous anger, I broke the first tablet of the law, so maybe I am being called back to Mt. Sinai for another.

But I can never be sure exactly what God has in mind. From burning bushes to bizarre plagues, I've learned that God is beyond figuring out.

These are the most unusual days I've ever lived, and from them I am getting to know God better—but it leaves me wanting more. So far, God has revealed only a glimpse of who He is. I am fascinated. I find myself longing to find another piece of the God-puzzle—something wonderful I've never known before. I long to see God's glory in this dismal place! My parched soul thirsts for God alone, as if I was created just to know Him.

I know that God wants me to lead the people on, but right now I don't know if I can do it anymore; leading a bunch of wild jackals would be easier! If I can just have another glimpse of God, it might make it easier; it might lift my heavy heart. Seeing God's glory will strengthen me, I just know it.

So I pray desperately, "Show me your glory." And in response, I see the most incredible thing I've ever seen:

In a cloud the Lord came down calling, "Yahweh! The Lord! The God of compassion and mercy! I am slow to anger and filled with unfailing love and faithfulness. I lavish unfailing love to a thousand generations. I forgive iniquity, rebellion, and sin. But I do not excuse the guilty. I lay the sins of the parents upon their children and grandchildren; the entire family is affected—even children in the third and fourth generations. (Exod. 34:5-8 NLT)

Even though I don't fully understand what I've seen in that God-cloud, I am awestruck by His glory and immediately throw myself to the ground in worship.

Moses was appalled when the people turned away from God and bowed down to a golden calf. He had taught them better. Hadn't they seen God's miracles? Moses had worked hard to make a difference, but in the end, nothing had changed. He felt angry and betrayed—like a colossal failure.

THE STORM OF DISAPPOINTMENT

We've all been there. We work hard and pray harder, but it doesn't seem to help. Sometimes we fail, even when we are trying to serve and follow God. Life lands a crushing blow right on our jaw, and we feel defeated and disillusioned. Everything goes terribly wrong, and we ask with clinched fists, "Why, Lord?"

Or at least I've done that before. Large-scale disaster hit me for the first time when I was in college. Unlike Moses, I was not on Mt. Sinai or in the desert. My life fell apart right in the middle of a thunderstorm in Auburn, Alabama.

I had been in a volatile, unhappy relationship with my longtime boyfriend. He had borrowed my car, and I suddenly decided at midnight that I wanted it back right then, even though a major storm was brewing. Angrily, I set out on foot to retrieve it. It was a crazy thing I just had to do, even in the rain and lightning.

I clutched my umbrella as I walked down a windy side street. I paused by the creaking iron gates of an old cemetery and considered my future. I was a college senior and would soon be on my own. As I stood there soaking wet, I realized this relationship was not right for either of us. I knew if I didn't walk away, my life would be filled with many stormy moments, just like this. I felt God leading me to break up and move on, without looking back.

But . . .

My whole future with him was already planned. Walking
away would be so painful. It meant completely starting over with
no plan, and worse, with no boyfriend.

As I huddled against the rough cemetery wall in the middle
of the storm, I felt the sting of disappointment and the blow
of defeat. It felt like my life was over. I asked all the typical
questions, like, "Why did you let me get hurt, Lord?" and "How
do you expect me to go on?" (By the way, those aren't the right
questions and they lead to nowhere.) When Moses's heart was
broken, he didn't ask "why me?" or "can I quit?" Rather, he
prayed, "Show me your glory." He surrendered to what had
happened and asked God to reveal Himself.

After my thunderstorm realization, I was resolute. I ended my
unhealthy relationship the very next day. Then, I spent a couple
of months wallowing in the pit of depression. I wish I had known
then about Moses's prayer and how God's glory can lift us out
of despair. Eventually, I did recover and God's blessings rained
down. The next year, I got engaged to my husband, Mike, and
we've been married for thirty years now.

I'm sure you've had your share of disappointment and
heartache too: a big order is canceled, your teenager gets
arrested, a job is lost, or a friend betrays. It knocks you down
for the count. Defeat discourages us. It dries us up inside. Our
creativity and enthusiasm for life evaporate like raindrops in the
desert. When the blow really hurts, it's hard to get motivated to
continue. When I am in the pits, I just want to lie in bed all day
in a flannel shirt and eat chocolate.

I think Moses might have wanted to do that too (that's a funny
picture, isn't it?). Moses's life had had some major setbacks. As
a prince, he had failed and was exiled. As a prophet, he hadn't

communicated well or inspired allegiance. He was a leader whose people went astray. I suspect he felt so disappointed and ineffective that he wanted to throw his staff down and walk off the job. (I would have.) But we can learn something valuable from Moses. He found a way to weather the storm of disappointment by asking God to show him something specific: His glory.

THE STAIRS OUT OF DESPAIR

Like a blinking beacon on the shore, God's glory gives us hope and inspiration to persevere through a storm. He is a fixed point in the chaos of life: the stops and starts, defeats and victories. When we get down, it's tempting to quit or stay defeated and not fulfill our calling. Moses shows us a unique way to become inspired again: we can find the courage to go on by seeking God's glory, as he did.

A glimpse of God's glory is a jumpstart, a catalyst that can quickly lift us up and propel us onward. It can do more for us than any self-help program or shrink. God had a special glory-ride for Moses, and it changed his life and the way he led. Seeing God's glory not only pulled Moses out of despair, but it changed his whole countenance in a way that others noticed: "When Moses came down from Mount Sinai with the two tablets of the covenant law in his hands, he was not aware that his face was radiant because he had spoken with the Lord. When Aaron and all the Israelites saw Moses, his face was radiant, and they were afraid to come near him" (Exod. 34:29-30). Moses's face became radiant (literally) after his encounter with God. It was as if God's glory was transferred to Moses both physically and spiritually.

Seeking God's glory can lead us out of despair and change our countenances too. God's glory lifts us up—it's a vacation from suffering. We can seek His glory in three specific ways: by looking up at who God is, by looking back at what He has done, and by looking ahead to what He will do. These are the stairs out of despair, and God's glory leads us up, step by step.

Stair 1: Looking Up

The first step up from discouragement and despair is to look up to God rather than to ourselves and what we think we need. When I first started learning to seek the glory of God, I soon discovered that I had a problem—I wanted some glory for me too. I felt like I deserved some recognition, yet my kids seemed to take me for granted. Mike seemed pretty unaware of all the wonderful things I did. No one fussed over me like they should have, and no one sang my praises enough. After all I did for other people, it seemed to me some applause and stroking were in order! Maybe you know someone like me.

But learning to appreciate God's glory made me realize that no one really owes me anything. Glory is owed to God, alone. That is a life principle: all glory is due to God; none is due to me. I struggle with wanting recognition and honor from others for what I do, but unlike me, the Apostle Paul didn't seem to. He said: "Whatever you do, work at it with all your heart, as though you were working for the Lord and not for people" (Col. 3:23 GNT).

Learning this showed me that Mike and the children don't owe me for what I *choose* to do for them. No thank-you notes or pats on the back are necessary for my well-being (although they're nice). My family doesn't need to live according to my whims and wishes to pay me back. I can't use my handy list of "all the sacrifices I make" to guilt them into action, because they do not owe me, they owe God.

This also means that my church doesn't owe me a plaque for

my wall or a letter of appreciation for serving. The PTA and
the garden club don't owe me flowers and a round of applause.
Serving in these places is my choice. Hopefully, I serve in a way
that honors God. When I don't need constant recognition, it frees
me to just be myself.

Serving to amplify God's glory produces peace and power.
Honoring God as much as possible suppresses our voracious
appetite for recognition, and it stops us from competing for
it. Fishing in "recognition pond" only leaves us anxious and
discontented because we can't ever catch enough (I've tried).
If recognition and importance had been Moses's motivation,
he wouldn't have made it. Moses did something extraordinary
because he did it for God, not himself. We, too, will do
extraordinary things when our motivation is to bring glory to
God.

Frankly, we will use our energy in one way or another. If it's
not used for making God look good, then it naturally shifts to
making us look good. Or our kids. Or our families. If we don't
look for ways to make God important, then rest assured, we will
look for ways to make *ourselves* look important. Feeding our
ego crowds out delighting in God's glory. Pride just takes up too
much room. Psalm 10:4 says, "In his pride the wicked man does
not seek him [God]; in all his thoughts there is no room for God."

Consider "Jackie," a new convert who came to our
neighborhood Bible study. She was an energetic young mother,
outspoken and completely without a filter. She often thought
out loud. One morning, she shook her blonde curly head with a
sigh and said, "God must be *really* insecure because He needs so
much attention. If God has everything, then why does He need so
much praise?"

Although she raised some eyebrows, Jackie had asked an

honest question. In fact, she had the nerve to question something that many of us have pondered from time to time. Later Jackie realized that God wasn't needy—she was. She told me, "When you love to be the center of attention, praising God seems trivial, like a waste of time. But it isn't. Now I understand why we do it—looking at Him instead of ourselves lifts our hearts!" Good for you, Jackie.

Failing to look up and praise God causes our mind's pendulum to swing toward us, making us so praise-needy that we resent glory going to anyone else—even to God. Glorifying God gives us balance and keeps us from falling into the pit of being our own god. Glorifying God as we seek Him doesn't help God—it helps us climb out of despair.

Stair 2: Looking Back

Seeking God's glory is even more than looking up and worshipping Him. It includes looking back at what He has done. More than two thousand years ago, God gave us His Son, Jesus Christ, and no gift has ever cost Him as much.

How would you feel if you sent your child far, far away—like, to Mars—for life? Would you experience a searing sense of loss? Feel wounded? Or suffer from separation anxiety? I wonder if those were some of the emotions God felt when Jesus came to earth. On a *much* lesser scale, I can relate. When Caroline, my oldest, left for college, I had some of those same feelings. My head hurt, my heart hurt, and even my bones hurt with sorrow. I remember being paralyzed by questions like, "How will I ever be happy again?" I lost the everyday joy of being with my child: the late-night conversations, laughing at our inside jokes, looking into her eyes. For eighteen years, she was with me every day. I went on her field trips and took her cheerleading group to practice. We had birthday parties and sleepovers. Then she was gone. And my home changed forever.

Tears streaked down my face as I walked one gray morning and prayed for comfort. The bleak sky seemed to mirror my inward gloom. I was running low on inspiration to do anything, so I prayed Moses's prayer, "Show me your glory on this dark day," and God did. He comforted me by giving me a spiritual blessing to outweigh my sorrow. He graced me with a vivid picture of how He felt when His Son left heaven. Here's what I saw:

Long ago, there was a circle of light. Three living beings were so enmeshed that it was hard to tell where one stopped and the other began. This circle of fellowship shone brightly before anything else existed. Like spokes in a wheel, the three spun as one circle. Their oneness was satisfying, beautiful, and complete. When they created the world, each played a separate role, yet they did it together.

One day, one of them ripped away and fell to the earth, taking on the form of His creation because He loved it so. When Jesus left the circle, it felt like muscle tearing away from bone. All three beings suffered the pain of separation and loss. Although they were united in heart, they were physically separated for the first time. Ever.

This separation was kind of like my daughter's and mine, but here is where it gets really different: the Father and Holy Spirit stayed spirits, but the Son took on flesh. And that changed the circle forever. Jesus became like His children in every way (Heb. 2:14, 17). To me, that means He was permanently altered for all time.

Yes, God understood my pain. But only now could I begin to

understand His. And the lesson wasn't over. God showed me that He and I are physically separated too. He feels the same pain of separation for *me*. He longs for the day when we will come face to face, when I come home to Him. He misses me like I miss Caroline. As I considered how God must feel, the bitter sting lifted and His glory comforted me in a way I don't really understand.

This circle of light lives inside of me, and you, and all who believe. We have joined the golden family circle, not merely as observers but as children who remain forever. When you have trouble seeking God's glory, start with that circle and you will end up on your knees.

Stair 3: Looking Ahead

Like a halo, God's glory encircles what He has done for you and me—He gave us His very best in Jesus Christ. He has also promised us a glorious future. We seek God's glory by looking ahead: someday, we will physically kneel before the Lord and see His glory in all its magnificence.

Imagine how this moment might look. Isaiah described the sight of God sitting on His throne in Isaiah 6:1, "I saw the Lord, high and exalted, seated on the throne; and the train of his robe filled the temple." Isaiah connects the temple and the throne room together here, so I assume the throne room looks somewhat like Solomon's temple did, for it was merely a copy of the true one in heaven.

Hebrews 10:20 says that Jesus opened up a new way for us to pass through the curtain or veil into this holy place. Let's walk through the torn veil and imagine what that could possibly be like.

As we enter the throne room, we brush past the linen curtain of blue, purple, and scarlet (2 Chron. 3:14). We walk across cool tiles of polished blue lapis (Exod. 24:10). The golden lampstands are

lit and their flickering light dances across golden walls (2 Chron.
3:5). The air smells like incense and the atmosphere is heavy
with awe and reverence. A large white throne (Rev. 20:11) sits in
a circle of light in the center of the room. Winged angels hover
in the glory around it. As we bow before God and the Son at His
right hand, we feel a rush of sheer joy, assured that this moment
is exactly what we were created for. In that moment, we receive
our reward and share of eternal glory (Rom. 8:17).

I used to think the pearly gates, streets of gold, and the
mansion over the hilltop were the rewards of salvation. But those
are only fringe benefits—mere building materials—and their
glory alone cannot satisfy. Spending eternity in the circle of light
with the Father, Son, and Holy Spirit is our ultimate reward, the
greatest possible joy.

Seeking God's glory now—glimpsing our future and
sampling our inheritance—is merely practicing for later on. How
good of God to give us a taste of future glory right now. Like
Moses, we get to see brief glimpses of God to strengthen and
help us while we are still far away from our future home. These
glimpses confirm where we are going. They can pull us out of
the pit of despair. Each time we seek God's glory, it enables us
to walk on with resolve, continuing our journey toward eternity
with Him.

THE GLORY OF GOD

If the glory of God had a color, it would be shimmering gold.

*If it were a picture, it would look like a
radiant, sparkling cloud of light.*

*If it had a sound, it would be more beautiful than a symphony;
more majestic than a million voices singing in harmony.*

If it had a taste, it would be sweet and fresh.

*If God's glory had a fragrance, it would smell pure,
like a pleasant, yet penetrating aroma.*

If it were a feeling, it would be heavy and powerful.

*It would have energy: a magnetic drawing that fills up and displaces
anything in its way.*

*Like light, it could travel with great speed, reaching and overcoming
any darkness in its path and illuminating everything it touches.*

*God's glory never ends. Like a ray of light
it beams on and on across miles, years, space, and eternity.*[1]

Seek and Find

1. Read and meditate on Exodus 34:1-8, 2 Corinthians 3:18, 2 Corinthians 4:6-9, and Psalm 34:8-10. According to these verses, why is it important to know what Scripture says about God's glory?

2. Why was it important for Moses to see God's glory at a time when he was discouraged? Describe a time when you felt discouraged and looked up at who God is, back at what He has done, and ahead to what He will do. If you didn't use these "stairs" to climb out of the pit, how might you have done so and what difference would it have made?

3. How have you been feeling lately? If it seems like you're having more than your share of disappointment or defeat, consider how glimpsing God's glory could affect your life, right now. In what situations might seeking God's glorious face affect your countenance and lift your heart?

4. Write about a time when you saw or experienced God's glory and what it meant to you. How can you keep this memory alive?

5. Consider areas where you might be seeking glory for yourself. Repent and lift your eyes to God's mesmerizing beauty. David said he longed to "gaze at the beauty of the Lord" (Ps. 27:4). May it be our longing and satisfaction as well.

6. Read Revelation 22:1-5. Journal or discuss with a group about the moment when you first kneel before the Lord's throne. Does my description of this moment (on pg.43-44) help you? What

would you change or add to it? What might this moment feel like? Envisioning our future gives us hope and renewed perspective.

CHAPTER 4

The Thief

Seeking Invites Grace

*Humility makes us ready to be blessed by the God of all grace,
and fits us to deal efficiently with our fellow-men.*

CHARLES SPURGEON

Monte Sano Mountain towers more than one thousand feet above
my hometown of Huntsville, Alabama. It is part of a chain of
mountains that beautifully defines the backdrop of our city. I
know the shape of each mountain by heart because I have lived
my entire life in the valley below. On the top of Monte Sano
stands a concrete and marble cross. My dad and I hiked up to the
base of it one time—it's huge. Visible for miles, the cross is a
loving reminder to me of home.

But that singular cross isn't really accurate. At the crucifixion
of Christ, there were three crosses—and I've always wondered
why. Wouldn't highlighting Jesus alone be better than muddying
up the water with criminals? Jesus could've had a solo act on

history's center stage, but strangely, He chose to share His death with two sinners.

Now I understand that there is an important lesson about salvation here. The thieves represent all mankind. We are either on one side of the cross or the other. On the left, we see a guilty man, full of arrogance, refusing to believe. On the right, we see another guilty man, but he humbles himself and accepts grace. The thieves display the only two responses there are to Jesus—pride or humility. There is no middle ground.

Our response to grace changes the course of our lives, just like it did for the thief on the cross.

A Thief Seeks

I never had a chance. I started out behind the eight ball and never caught up. Born into poverty and raised on the streets, I have stolen for as long as I can remember. I am really a pretty good person at heart; mostly I just steal what I need. Maybe sometimes I take a bit extra, but there are worse people out there than me. If our society were more just, I would have had more opportunities. With very few choices in life, I turned to crime.

Now the music has stopped and I have no chair left. I was caught stealing, again, but the killing part was purely an accident. It doesn't matter now because I am hanging on a cross, living while dying, with no hope of anything more.

I am not alone; my accomplice is hanging with me and, strangely, so is a Jewish rabbi. It's kind of a cruel irony, crucifying a holy man alongside lowlifes like us. Many are mocking Him, with words as hard and cold as ice. Surely, there is no mercy in this place. It's dark; death and hatred hang in the air. In contrast, the rabbi is gentle, humble, and kind. I doubt He deserves this; He isn't guilty—like I am.

The rabbi says, "Forgive them, Father, for they know not what they do." The tone of the words shatters my heart into a million pieces. Words raw and selfless, releasing love into this atmosphere of death. He should be angry at the terrible injustice; how can He pardon His murderers? I see Him now as if for the first time, hanging there as if He bore the weight of the world upon His shoulders.

Maybe He really is the Son of God, as I've heard Him called. No one else could bring light into this present darkness. As the painful hours go by, the more I see light, the more I believe. No one has taught me this—somehow truth has been revealed to me. Being in His presence makes me different.

My friend mocks Him, sarcastically daring the rabbi to save us all. I use my labored breaths to jump to His defense: "We deserve to die, but this man has done nothing wrong. Remember me, Lord, when you come into your kingdom." He replies with words that speak life into my dying heart: "Today, you will be with me in Paradise."

Suddenly I have hope, something I have never had before. I did nothing to deserve this, nothing but believe that Jesus is the Christ. The cross is the best, worst thing that has ever happened to me. I have lived an evil life, but He has shown me grace. Today I will die, but I will be with the Son of God either way.

An old saying comes to mind, and I realize it is talking about me: "Surely your goodness and love will be with me all of my life, and I will live in the house of the LORD forever" (Ps. 23:6 NCV). Someday heaven could rightly be called a den of thieves, but most likely it will be called the home of those made righteous, like you and I.

The story of the thief is our story, if we are believers in Christ. We are the thief. We were dying. We had no hope or future. We were unworthy. We gave our guilt to Christ and took His innocence.

The thief knew he did not deserve grace, yet he reached out to Jesus anyway. As a result, he was granted eternal life and a sense of assurance in the midst of dire circumstances. When he sought Jesus and humbly accepted grace, he was saved. He didn't have to qualify. He didn't have to do a bunch of good works or perfectly obey the law. Neither do we. Like the thieves, we either respond to the cross in humble faith or in arrogance. We are either spiritually dead or alive. Saved or not. Because of what Jesus did for us on the cross, we are invited into the grace of God's presence. Spending time there gives life, light, and hope in darkness.

GRACE LIFTS US UP

For years, I had no understanding of grace, so I was never sure if I was saved. When I was young, a misguided Sunday school teacher taught our class to be sure to repent of the day's sins at bedtime every night so we would be forgiven in case we died in our sleep. That's a pretty heavy message for seven-year-olds, isn't it? I sat there in my little green plastic chair, staring at the felt board, weighed down with the fear of God's wrath toward bad children. After that, I tried to repent at bedtime for each fight I had had with my little brother that day —which was pretty difficult to keep straight. Anxiously, I repented for accidents, like stepping on the cat's tail, and for pre-meditated sins like stealing my sister's chocolate. And then I would commit similar sins the next day.

While this may have led me to develop some good scorekeeping skills, it also instilled a growing sense of spiritual insecurity in me because I never felt good enough—for God,

man, or myself. Maybe you have felt that way. The problem with
spiritual insecurity is that it bleeds into all areas of life. Inwardly,
I felt anxious and lacking, so I tried to make myself feel better
by comparing and competing with others. I used to live life
constantly looking for people, good scores, and compliments to
prop me up. This is a pretty self-centered and unhappy way to live.

Thankfully, the thief didn't focus on how he felt. He didn't
let his unworthiness stop him from seeking Jesus. He focused on
who Jesus was and humbly accepted grace. It's the same for you
and me. Instead of focusing on how we feel or perform, we can
concentrate on seeking the Lord over and over. We have a choice.
We can spend time meditating on God's promises or rehearsing
our inadequacies. We can seek to grasp the gospel story or be all
about our own story. We can ignore the gift of grace or we can
learn to rejoice in it every day. Grace lifts us up. It's the cure for
feeling insecure.

This verse really helped me to accept grace: "Very truly I tell
you, whoever hears my word and believes him who sent me has
eternal life and will not be judged but has crossed over from death
to life" (John 5:24). We are not "good enough"—*but we don't
have to be*. Christ was good for us. When we believe, we inherit
eternal life and cross over to a better and more fulfilling life in the
here and now. The gospel reveals that God thinks you and I are
worth saving. What great news! Meditating on this truth daily has
helped me build a more positive self-image, transforming the way
I think and live.

GRACE FLOWS THROUGH US

God wants us to humbly delight in the gift of grace every day. But
grace is not ours alone to revel in. The blessing of God's mercy
is not supposed to stop with you or me. At Calvary, we see grace

flowing away from the prideful man and showering the lowly one. This teaches us that pride repels grace, but humility attracts it. The humble heart allows the current of grace to pass through it to others.

Writer Anne Lamott illustrates this idea: "The Gulf Stream will flow through a [drinking] straw, provided the straw is aligned to the Gulf Stream."[1] In other words, something vast and powerful can flow through us, if we are willing to humbly align ourselves with it. God wants to use us as unique channels for His grace, as He did with Jesus. He can send grace through us to hard-to-reach people. The more humble we become, the more grace flows (1 Pet. 5:5). But humility is really unnatural for us (sorry). That's why we often struggle to give grace out. This is certainly my struggle. After receiving with joy all the wonderful aspects of grace, mercy, and forgiveness, sometimes I'm not very eager to extend them to others. I can easily let grace stop with me.

Once a client named "Dwight" stormed into my office with an angry scowl and a red face. His bright green sweater and rapid pacing reminded me of a green horsefly buzzing angrily back and forth before it stings. As he talked, his eyes seemed to bulge out like an insect's.

He was my first angry client. I felt like a deer startled by headlights, and I couldn't think of much to say. I was a rookie, fresh out of college, and totally caught off-guard. He called me a name I can't mention here, and he accused me of things I didn't know anything about.

Of course, after Dwight left, I thought of many "colorful" responses. I told him off in my head over and over. The gross injustice angered me. I didn't know why I had been subjected to his rant. Eventually, I got to the bottom of the problem: he thought I had lied to him. But before I could give him a piece of my mind, he came to my office and apologized for misjudging me. I told him he was forgiven—but, honestly, that was a stretch. I held on to that offense for years. I told and retold the story, emphasizing what an idiot Dwight was. One day I saw him out running with his dog. The dog yanked him off balance and he fell forward like a downhill skier, his arms and legs flying—and I enjoyed it immensely. Years later, I realized that I had actually treated Dwight worse than he had treated me.

Extending grace requires humility—and my lack of it was my problem. I thought I was a better person than Dwight. After all, I would never be so rude or unfair. Except . . . I had lied about forgiving him and said ugly things behind his back. I had compared him to a stinging horsefly, which wasn't quite fair. I've learned that an ugly response is often much worse than throwing the first punch.

When I think of the gospel and of all the grace Jesus gives me for mistakes like that, I realize that I am not above committing any sin. If I excel in one area, rest assured, I will fail in another. It's good for me (and you) to understand that we need grace as much as Dwight or the thief does. And since I have received grace, I am obligated to humbly let it pass through me to people like Dwight.

PRIDE AND HUMILITY

Extending grace requires daily, sacrificial, and sometimes painful humility. But what does humility actually look like? The chart on the following page offers some examples of the contrast between pride and humility.

Writing this list of prideful statements was easy because I've probably said just about all of them at one time or another.

PRIDE	HUMILITY
"God is not always fair. Sometimes He's cruel and unjust."	"God loves mercy and justice. I can trust in His goodness, even when I can't see it."
"I never, ever lie . . ."	"I want to tell the truth, but I am very capable of lying, given the right situation."
"I can rely on myself. I am a good person."	"God alone is good. I can trust Him, not myself."
"Grace, or sinners getting off the hook, makes me uncomfortable, so I avoid talking about it."	"I am overwhelmed by the grace God has given to me. Let's talk about it!"
"I separate myself and shut out those who are different from me. I label others."	"I try to remove barriers, include and respect others. I value unity, so I avoid labeling."
"What about me?"	"You go first."
"I know I'm right! You are so wrong!"	"I honestly believe I'm right, but I could be wrong. I've been wrong before."
"I'm stressed out, so it's understandable if I lash out at others. My impatience is okay."	"When I'm stressed, it's wrong for me to make others suffer. Impatience and lashing out aren't okay."
"It's not my fault! I can't help it! If everybody did what they were supposed to this wouldn't have happened."	"I'm so sorry. Please forgive me. Let me make it right."
"I know what I need to know. I don't intend to change."	"I love to learn. I can recount specifically what I've learned or how I've changed lately."

Rooting out pride isn't a very fun process, but hopefully this chart will inspire you to identify ways that pride may be keeping you from extending grace to others.

GRACE THROUGH KATIE

My friend "Katie" models grace flowing through humility so beautifully. When I think about being a channel of grace, remembering her story helps me grasp it a little better. Maybe it will help you too.

Katie's bright smiling face, sparkling green eyes, and cute designer jeans could fool you into thinking her life was easy. But actually, it's been pretty hard. Her life shifted tragically when her mom died from cancer when Katie was six. Katie suffered overwhelming grief that was too heavy for a little child bear. Soon, she couldn't remember much about her mother—the last year had been a blur of stark hospital rooms and awkward visits. Katie remembers more about her mom's death than her life. She can still recall the pungent smell of mildew and flowers in the creepy funeral home. She remembers how cold it was at the graveyard. She remembers being confused about where her mother had gone. It was a horrible time, but soon, it got much worse.

Within two years, Katie's irresponsible dad put her in foster care. She moved to rural Georgia to live in a doublewide with a large, rowdy foster family. It was a grueling transition. She received meager care and even less love. At night, she would lie there and try to remember what it felt like to have parents—but she couldn't. All she could feel was the sting of abandonment— her mom had died and her dad had given her away.

After two years in a painful foster situation, Katie's Aunt Ella came and got her. She moved Katie into her home. Ella took her to church and read the Bible to her at the breakfast table. Grace reached Katie through Ella, and it saved her.

Later, God gave Katie what she wanted most—a family of her own and friends who truly love her (including me). For years, her immediate family consisted of a husband, two children, and one very sick, elderly father. Over the years, I've watched Katie cancel vacations, move her dad to various nursing homes, and argue over insurance claims to get him the right medicine—all for a hurtful parent who still didn't love her, even in his old age.

Watching Katie care for her father was a bit like sitting on the front row at Calvary and watching grace rain down on a totally undeserving thief. She avoided retaliating or walking away, even as he was cussing her out or swinging a fist. I've never seen anything like it. Somehow, she kept on humbly serving the father who had abandoned her until the day he died. I was there. As he approached death in a small nursing home in Franklin, Tennessee, Katie told him about the cross and the grace that runs down from it. Katie prayed with him, and I assume that when he passed from this life, he came alongside another undeserving guy, the thief on the cross, who was saved by the same grace. Like a stream, Christ's grace ran to Ella, and on to Katie, and then to her dad. Year after year, visit after visit, the river of grace ran on and on. It was my blessing to stand on the bank and witness it.

Just like the thief, we meet grace at the cross. This is why it's so important to focus often on Christ's story—it invites us to enter that grace. Part of seeking to know the Lord is striving to better grasp and appreciate what He did for us. Doing this daily changes our lives. His grace runs red from the cross straight into our hearts, and then slowly—sometimes painfully—it moves through the channel of our lives to others.

Meditating on what Christ did for us enables grace to shape

our lives and our futures in a powerful way. It gives us amazing strength to love and serve others. If we let grace flow through us, it will come back around and bless us further. As we seek to grasp the gospel story, we will find the Lord to be very near.

1. Consider the following verses as you seek to grasp Christ's gift of grace. Rewrite these promises in your own words. What exactly has God done for you through His love and grace?

"He personally carried our sins in his body on the cross so that we can be dead to sin and live for what is right. By his wounds you are healed" (1 Pet. 2:24 NLT).

"But because of his great love for us, God, who is rich in mercy, made us alive with Christ even when we were dead in transgressions—it is by grace you have been saved" (Eph. 2:4-5).

2. What aspect of the gospel story is most meaningful to you? Why?

3. Review the pride and humility chart. Which statement is the most significant, challenging, or amusing to you? Why?

4. Read the following verses aloud:

"Live a life filled with love, following the example of Christ. He loved us and offered himself as a sacrifice for us, a pleasing aroma to God" (Eph. 5:2 NLT).

"A new command I give you: Love one another. As I have loved you, so you must love one another" (John 13:34).

How did Katie extend God's grace? How can you? What actions
or attitudes in your life might prevent someone from knowing
and experiencing God's grace?

5. List specific ways you can extend grace to others in your
current circumstances this week.

CHAPTER 5

Mary of Bethany:

Seeking Fills Us with God's Love

My love isn't a weapon, it's a lifeline, reach out and take hold, and don't let go!

FRANCINE RIVERS

I once heard a landscaper jokingly dub my mother the "queen of boxwoods." He was spot on—ancient boxwoods surrounded our house, outlining every bed and sidewalk. On hot, dry summer days the "queen" often sent her loyal subjects (my sister Lisa and me) out to water the boxwoods by hand.

One sticky, overcast afternoon, I was really tired of watering. I held the hose, swatting at mosquitoes and praying for rain. God must have been listening, because soon it began to pour. By the time we turned off the water and rolled up the hoses, we were soaked. Excitedly, we sprinted up the porch stairs and paused to catch our breath.

"Look at the boxwoods!" Lisa whispered. "That's so weird." Rain drummed against the roof as we stood on the porch, mesmerized, watching the giant, green boxwoods visibly relax their branches. It looked like the bushes were slowly opening their arms wide to receive water from above. Fat raindrops quickly saturated the thick outer layer of leaves, and then soaked the inward branches. Finally, the rain began to pool around their shallow, tangled roots.

We were delighted! We gave each other high-fives and raced back into the house. We knew the heavy rain would sustain the boxwoods for days.

It's kind of like that for us, spiritually, too. Like the boxwoods, our souls need to open up and drink in God's love, His *living* water, in order to thrive. Part of seeking to know God includes opening our hearts to receive His love, daily. The knowledge of His love can be stored in our souls (Rom. 5:5), like water is stored in a jar, filling us until it overflows to others.

Of course, most of us know (intellectually) that God loves us. Some of us grew up singing songs about it in Sunday school. We read about God's love in the Bible and even on billboards and bumper stickers. We often tell others that God loves them. But do we really grasp it?

I don't, always.

When I feel like nobody cares about me, it's easy to forget that God cares. A bout of anxiety can leave me feeling like God must be leaning back in His easy chair, totally unaware of my troubles. When someone treats me harshly, it's easy to wonder if God might be a bit harsh too. When I fail to love others, it's difficult for me to imagine that God still loves me just the same as He did yesterday and will tomorrow.

In Ephesians 3, Paul admits that comprehending God's love

isn't easy. He prays that God will help the Ephesians (and us) grasp it: ". . . May your roots go down deep into the soil of God's marvelous love; and may you be able to *feel and understand*, as all God's children should, how long, how wide, how deep, and how high his love really is; and to experience this love for yourselves, though it is so great that you will never see the end of it or fully know or understand it . . ." (Eph. 3:17-19 TLB, emphasis mine). Paul wants us to *experience* God's love, even though we can't fully grasp it, because this helps us take hold of the reality in which every child of God lives. This is the truth that sets us free. God's love helps us live and love differently. A growing sense of being loved colors our minds and attitudes. The more we store His love away in our hearts, the more we have to give away.

Mary of Bethany sought to know Jesus's love. The first time the Bible mentions Mary, she sits at the feet of Jesus, seeking to grasp His love with her heart wide open.

— *Mary of Bethany Seeks* —

I watch the sun rise as I lean back against the trunk of an ancient olive tree. Birds hop from limb to limb, singing with all their might, and my heart sings with them. I have so much to be grateful for. My father, once known as "Simon, the leper," is no longer a leper. Jesus of Nazareth healed him with a single touch. After that, Father became a disciple, traveling throughout the country with Jesus, preparing for the kingdom of God to come.

My older brother Lazarus runs our household, now. When Jesus, Father, and the disciples passed through Bethany last year, they stayed with us. That visit transformed my life. Even though I'm the youngest and least important member of our household, Jesus seemed to really care about me. He asked me questions and told me wonderful stories. Like a fragrance, an overwhelming sense of His love lingered with me for weeks, changing the way I saw my life.

Tonight, Jesus and His disciples will visit again. I can't wait. All day long my sister Martha and I have been working in the kitchen, preparing a great feast. As I see the loaves of bread rising in the stone oven, my anticipation rises too. I begin dancing around the room, excitedly twirling Martha around with me.

"Stop acting so childish, Mary," she growls. But I can't help it. The most important man in the entire world is coming to our house, and I sense that He is looking forward to seeing me too.

Father arrives early. With a sparkle in his eye, he works along with us, telling stories about his adventures with Jesus. Martha and I exchange surprised glances—Father has never helped us in the kitchen before. Like his leprosy, his former prideful spirit has vanished and a new man has emerged. For the first time, I realize that Jesus's touch healed more than Father's body—it also healed his soul.

At last, the others arrive. When Jesus walks into our home, I am drawn to Him like a moth to a flame. I sit, totally mesmerized, hanging on His words as if my life depends on hearing them. And somehow, I know it does.

Martha glares at me from across the courtyard, motioning for me to come back to the kitchen. She needs me to help her, but I need to remain still and listen. Martha is concerned about the feast, but even more so about my dignity—it's improper for a young woman to sit and talk with the men—but I don't care. Finally, Martha complains to Jesus.

To my surprise He defends me, saying, "My dear Martha, you are worried and upset over all these details! There is only one thing worth being concerned about. Mary has discovered it, and it will not be taken away from her" (Luke 10:41-42 NLT).

Yes, I have discovered something better. Jesus's love frees me
to live beyond the stiff traditions my sister is trying to impose
on me. I'm inspired to love freely and openly. I sit before Him,
basking in His love, opening my soul and drinking it in like
living water. Jesus nods at me in approval and the expression in
His dark eyes seems to say, "Live in my love every day, Mary.
Continue to seek my face. Make the most of every opportunity
you have."

Later, we learn that Mary of Bethany had the privilege of
anointing Jesus. None of the men with Him understood it, but
she knew what she was doing. Some scoffed at her. Others even
rebuked her. Who did she think she was? Only high priests
are suitable to anoint kings. But in the Lord's unconventional
way, He called Mary, a lowly young woman from the shabby
little village of Bethany, for a great purpose. Jesus said to the
detractors, "Why are you bothering her? She has done a beautiful
thing to me. The poor you will always have with you, and you
can help them any time you want. But you will not always have
me. She did what she could. She poured perfume on my body
beforehand to prepare for my burial. Truly I tell you, wherever
the gospel is preached throughout the world, what she has done
will also be told, in memory of her" (Mark 14:6-9).

LIVING LOVED

Experiencing God's love daily enables us to live like we're loved.
Well-loved people love others. Loved people are free. Loved
people have hope. What a tragedy it is to be loved like this and
to still act unloved. I know. I can look back now at the years I

wasted by living as if God didn't really love me. Not focusing upward caused me to focus inward. This kept me feeling ungrateful and striving for more. Not feeling accepted hamstrung my life. Praise God, I don't have to live this way! And neither do you. We can be filled with God's love every day.

Or not. Even after knowing this, God's love can still be hard to grasp or feel, especially when we're down or discouraged. When I start feeling unloved and empty, I've discovered three secrets to living loved that help me fill up on God's love, over and over again.

Secret #1: Picturing It

A picture of a padlock, locked on a bridge railing, is pinned to a burlap-covered message board in my kitchen. A red heart is painted on the lock and the key is missing. "You are forever mine!" (Isa. 43:1) is written in decorative lettering beside the lock. This picture reminds me that no matter how I feel, God's love is locked on me. Let me explain.

In 2012, my daughter Caroline and I noticed a bunch of padlocks randomly attached to the railing of the Pont des Arts Bridge in Paris, France. We learned that couples write their names on padlocks and lock them to the bridge. Then, as a romantic gesture, they throw the key into the Seine River below. While this is meant to represent lasting commitment, I've read that many of these "love locked" couples didn't last.

While everlasting love is hard for us to give, we all want to receive it. We ache for it. We seek permanence in every loving relationship that we have. Perhaps this need drove more and more couples to add padlocks until the bridge began to buckle under their weight. In 2015, the heavy locks had to be removed, as if to prove how temporary our love can be.

When I start feeling unloved by family and friends and, ultimately, God, it's comforting to look over at the picture on my bulletin board. It reminds me that God's love is locked on me, no matter how I might feel. His love is a forever kind of love. Men can't remove it. Wars can't sever it. In fact, nothing in all creation will ever be able to separate us from the love of God (Rom. 8:39). This is our reality, but some days that can be pretty hard to absorb. Picturing God's love with a concrete, tangible image helps me. I have made several different "love pictures" with a Scripture, like this one. They grace the fridge, my closet shelving, and the pockets of my journal. This interjects this abstract, unseen truth into my everyday life.

Secret #2: Saying It out Loud

In addition to picturing God's love, it's also helpful to simply say, "God loves me," out loud. King David came up with this idea (not me), encouraging us to proclaim God's love every morning (Ps. 92:2). Speaking this truth out loud to our family and friends can help us build our understanding of God's love and help us extend it to others.

It's beneficial for our ears to hear truth because we sure do hear a lot of lies. Consider the outrageous claims advertisers make. In 2009, the Kellogg's cereal company claimed that eating Cocoa Krispies would "boost a child's immunity." The FTC issued warnings until this claim was removed from their ads. Volkswagen designed software to deceive Americans into thinking their diesel cars had low emissions. In 2005, sellers of Exercise in a Bottle were banned from marketing their false weight-loss products by a federal judge. And the lies continue.

Most of us expect advertisers to make false claims from time to time, but there is a great deceiver who is much more effective.

Satan whispers lies into our minds at just the right moments. Often, when we are tired, feeling weak or blue, a faint thought flickers across our minds, saying, "Nobody cares about you." Ever hear that one? Me, too! Maybe Mary (and possibly Martha) heard that lie as well.

Sometimes Satan whispers, "You're all alone!" While we know that God will never leave us, it can be tempting to entertain this thought. Basically, all of Satan's lies center on one central lie: "God doesn't really, *really* love you." If the deceiver can get us to believe this, he can render us ineffective. He can chain us up in fear. His lies can trap us in a pit of despair and take away our hope. God's enduring love is the one thing the evil one doesn't ever want us to feel or know.

Satan tempted Eve in the Garden of Eden with this same kind of lie: "You won't really die [if you eat the forbidden fruit]" (Gen. 3:4). Satan implied that God didn't love Eve enough to tell her the truth. Satan went on further to imply that God was trying to withhold the blessing of knowledge from her. Eve fell for it, and eventually we all do.

Saying, "God loves me" out loud, with confidence and enthusiasm, quickly dispels many of the lies we are tempted to believe. It's good to say it to your children. Tell it to your friends. Even your dog might benefit from an injection of truth every so often! The more we say this fact out loud, the better. We will come closer to believing it. Truth spoken out loud trickles down into the way we think and live.

The Apostle John spoke about this truth, referring to himself several times in the book of John as "the disciple whom Jesus loved." I've heard Bible teachers joke about this, saying, "John must have thought he was pretty special." But it's nothing to joke about, John was special because Jesus loved him—and so was Mary. And so are you and I.

Secret #3: Believe It

The third secret to living loved is to believe it—to know and understand how God sees us and why He chooses to love us, even though we may feel unlovable or undeserving.

When we put our faith in Jesus, He comes to live within our hearts (Gal. 2:20). That means Christ's life is hidden in ours. We don't have to deserve God's love or work for it. We are the recipients of a brand-new heart, as foretold in Ezekiel 36:26. When God sees us, He sees Jesus shining within us.

While I know this is true, the enormity of this gift can be pretty hard to take in. If I'm not seeking God's love, the "old, old, story" can just grow old, fading like yesterday's newspaper. God has given me an unforgettable picture of what Christ living in me means. In fact, remembering Ty Osman II, my friend's son, helps me know that God loves me in an incredible way. Maybe it will help you know it too.

ALWAYS CONNECTED

Nothing is small in Texas, especially sunsets. In fact, if you're heading west on I-30 toward Dallas at the end of the day, the colors can paint that big Texas sky so vividly that it's hard to see anything else. Against that blazing orange, objects can fade to black.

The Texas sun was just beginning to set when Ty Osman II pulled over to the side of I-30 to help a stranger who was involved in an accident. As he walked back toward his truck, he was hit by a passing car. The driver, blinded by the blazing sunset, never even saw him. Eighteen-year-old Ty was airlifted to the nearest hospital in critical condition.

His parents, Ty Sr. and Nancy, and his sisters, Adair and Kendall, flew in from Nashville that night. They stayed at his bedside for two days. Monitors beeped. Tests were run. There wasn't much the doctors could do. Young Ty never regained consciousness. On Sunday morning, March 4, 2012, he passed quietly from this life while his mother held his hand.

Ty had designated that he would like to be an organ donor, so his family graciously donated his organs. This decision altered the lives of five recipients forever. Five people received new life from his life.

A year later, the Osmans made the bittersweet trip back to Texas to meet the recipients of their son's organs. Nancy said, "We felt so blessed to meet them. We wanted to honor Ty's life in them. You never think you can feel such happiness and sorrow at the same time, but you can."[1]

The family listened to Ty's heart with a stethoscope. When it was Nancy's turn, she tearfully laid her head against the chest of the man who received Ty's heart and listened for a long time—she just wanted to feel close to her son again. Nancy had heard that heartbeat before: on the ultrasound machine before Ty was born, when she held him as a child, and even on the monitor for the last two days of his life. Now it beat on in someone else.

When I asked Nancy how she felt when she first met the recipient of Ty's heart, her green eyes filled with tears. "Part of my son was there! A part of him lives in that man . . . all I could feel toward him was joy and overwhelming love. We will always be connected."

How beautiful the love of a mother and a father is! God loves every believer like that. Much like Ty's heart lives on in another man, the heart of God's Son lives within us. When we receive Christ, He comes to dwell within our hearts. So when God looks at us, He sees His Son's life in us.

Consider what this means:

- God wants the best for us, and does not want to harm us (Jer. 29:11).
- God works for our good; He wants to bless us (Rom. 8:28).
- God listens intently to us, collecting our prayers in golden bowls (Rev. 5:8) and our tears in His bottle (Ps. 56:8 NLT).
- We will always be connected to God because of Christ in us (Heb. 9:15).

Sometimes, it seems like God must have lost our addresses or even forgotten our names. We can wonder if He has thrown up His hands and left us behind. Painful days can make us feel like God couldn't possibly love us anymore. When I feel like that, it helps me to remember Ty's story and know that these feelings aren't true. God's Son lives in us. We are precious in His sight.

Ty cherished God's love. Maybe he first saw it in the way his family loved him. He tweeted this verse, just days before his death, as if he knew what was coming:

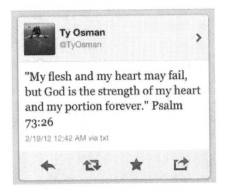

Ty Osman
@TyOsman

"My flesh and my heart may fail, but God is the strength of my heart and my portion forever." Psalm 73:26

2/19/12 12:42 AM via txt

God's love was Ty's strength and portion (or inheritance) forever, and it is ours too. The way Ty's parents still love him points toward a much greater love: the love God has for each of us. When we seek God's familiar face, we seek the face of One who loves us. We need to know we are loved. Every. Single. Day.

Seek His love by picturing it, saying it out loud, and believing it to be true, even when you might not be feeling it. God's love is locked on you, forever.

Seek and Find

Do you have difficulty saying, *"I'm the one Jesus loves?"*
Consider these verses as you reflect on God's love for you. Write
your name in the blanks, and read them aloud.

1. Jesus prayed: *"I have given _____ the glory you
gave me, so that _____ may be one with us as we
are one. I am in _____ and you are in me. May
_____ experience such perfect unity that the world
will know that you sent me and that you love _____
as much as you love me" (John 17:22-23 NLT).*

Write a short prayer thanking God for loving you as much as He
loves His own Son.

2. Discuss Ty Osman II's story with a friend or a group. What
new insight does it give you about the Spirit of Christ living
within your heart? What does this mean to you? What privileges,
blessings, and strengths does this indwelling bring to your life?

3. God said, *"Can a mother forget her nursing child? Can she
feel no love for the child she has borne? But even if that were
possible, I would not forget _____! See, I have
written your name (_____) on the palms of my
hands" (Isa. 49:15-16 NLT).*

How has God demonstrated His love for you in the past? Journal
or share about a time when God displayed His love to you.
Describe what it means to you that your name is written on

God's hands. Discuss the comfort and strength you get from this verse with a friend.

4. *"God is love. _____ who leads a life of love is joined to God. And God is joined to _____"*
(1 John 4:16 NIRV).

Pin this verse on your bulletin board. Read it aloud, often.

What does being joined to God mean to you? What promises, benefits, and blessings are associated with belonging to God?

5. What does leading a life of love mean? Break this concept down to the most meaningful people in your life. List and discuss specific ways you can share God's love with:

Your spouse:

Your family:

Your friends:

Your church family:

6. God never forgets to love us, yet we often forget to express our love back to Him. Saying the words, "I love you, Lord," several times a day out loud, can remind us to love God actively. Name some other specific ways you can express your love and gratitude back to God this week.

CHAPTER 6

Zacchaeus

Seeking Frees Us from Bondage

The God who made us can remake us.

WOODROW KROLL

I feel fortunate to know an Elvis impersonator—not everybody does. Mitchell Brown manages a brick and stone company. He is a quiet, good-hearted family man. There is nothing pretentious or showy about him. But let him don a white rhinestone-studded suit and he suddenly becomes "the King." I've never seen anything like it. Boy, for a churchgoer, Mitchell has some rhythm and moves! He exudes charisma and stage presence. His voice is a spot-on match. He has even won some national awards for his Elvis impersonation.

While Mitchell could easily land a job in Vegas, he uses his "Elvis talents" to raise money for local charities. It is so fun to watch Mitchell's remarkable transformation—he *is* the King. Sometimes it makes me laugh when I realize that I am kind of like him—I am an impersonator too. Aren't you? Don't all believers try to be like Jesus? We impersonate *the* King of kings.

Obviously, we can't impersonate Christ as well as Mitchell impersonates Elvis—we are only a weak representation, at best. But sometimes Jesus helps us imitate Him pretty well. He gives us a shining costume, a robe of righteousness to wear, and fills us with His Spirit. Then we can go out and bless other people. Miraculously, we shine and sparkle as reflections of Christ, giving light to the world.

Think that's a stretch? Look around. All the love you see has its origin in the Creator. When we put our arms around a crying child, we act like God. When we serve social outcasts, like Zacchaeus, a despised tax collector, we look a lot like Jesus. When we pray for and encourage each other in our faith, the Holy Spirit shines through us. And even though we fall short, a poor imitation of the King is still beautiful.

Zacchaeus became an impersonator too. His belief in Christ released him *from* the chains of greed *to* a second chance. Zacchaeus began to act like the King. While we aren't told very much about Zacchaeus, I can imagine why he *might* have sought out Jesus.

Zacchaeus Seeks

Most people on the streets of Jericho avoid making eye contact with me. Some consider me a traitor. Others know I'm ruthless. All of them owe taxes and will have to deal with me, sooner or later. I can be a "creative" tax collector when people can't pay— that's why the Romans hired me. I really don't care where the tax money comes from or where it goes, as long as some of it lands in my pocket. Now I have an entire staff collecting for me, and business is booming. People here can afford to be squeezed.

Some jealously call me "new money" because I purchase every bell and whistle I want. I have a sparkling ring on every finger. My Italian leather sandals are stacked to make me look taller. A thick golden chain is laced through my red cloak—I almost have the bearing of a god among these peasants! I sneer as I walk by people on the street. I know they hate me and I will never have many friends, but I have cash, and that's enough.

Almost.

Recently, my wife left me. And even though I've spoiled my children, they seem to despise me. Now, even my mistress has left me for a Roman official. For the first time in my life, I'm feeling strange pangs of regret and guilt. I keep longing for something more. For all that I own, sometimes I feel like I have nothing at all. I need to make some sort of change, but I don't know how.

A man on the street corner announces that Jesus, the great prophet of Nazareth, is passing through Jericho. I've heard mysterious stories about Jesus's miracles and profound wisdom. Maybe I can pay Him to help me find inner peace and happiness.

Crowds gather as Jesus walks down the street, but I can't see Him. As usual, there are too many people in my way. *If only I were taller. How many times have I secretly wished this? Never more than today.* So, I toss my fine sandals and cloak aside and climb a large sycamore tree to see what I can see. I know it's undignified—a wealthy man climbing a tree like a squirrel—and I even surprise myself when I go out on a limb to seek after Jesus.

As Jesus passes by me, I sense His power. I'm somehow drawn to this man, as if I have known Him before. Abruptly, Jesus turns around and says, "Zacchaeus!" But how does Jesus know me? This highly respected rabbi says He wants to go to *my* house, a place no one wants to go anymore. I feel honored, and a bit sheepish, as I climb down and walk with Jesus.

My servants prepare a great feast of roasted lamb and fine wine for us. When Jesus speaks, it's as if His words are alive.

Instinctively, I know what He says is true. Suddenly everything changes as I realize this about myself: I'm physically rich, but spiritually poor. Jesus is poor, yet rich because He finds His treasure in God. This is real freedom. I see now that I've been in bondage for years, chasing wealth and happiness to no fulfilling end. Now, I want to be free more than I've ever wanted anything.

As I spend the day with Jesus, I learn that His freedom could be mine. I tell Him that I will gladly make amends for the money I've stolen. His face shines as He proclaims: "Salvation has come to this home today, for this man has shown himself to be a true son of Abraham. For the Son of Man came to seek and save those who are lost" (Luke 19:9-10 NLT).

Just like Zacchaeus, when we seek the Lord, we find Him. Being in His presence makes us inwardly rich. It brings freedom and fullness of joy that transcends our circumstances. God gives us spiritual sight, and it changes us permanently. After a while, we discover that we really weren't doing all the seeking; we were the ones being sought.

SEARCHING FOR TREASURE

How did Zacchaeus go from reaching for money to reaching for God? His change of heart started with a simple action. Zacchaeus *physically* positioned himself in a tree in order to seek the Lord. What about you? Are you physically positioning yourself? When have you tried doing something uncomfortable in order to know God better? When have you turned off the TV, left the dirty dishes in the sink, and chosen to spend time with the Lord instead? Do you have so much to do that being with Him feels . . . well, less important? I get it.

Every time I speak, I ask the audience if they struggle to find time to spend with the Lord daily. Almost everyone in the room raises his or her hand. That indicates there may be some needy, starving souls out there. Someone's spiritual tank is running on empty. Hearts may be growing cold and frosting over. Maybe some are so hungry for God that their soul growls like a lion that hasn't been fed much in a week or two. Or six. Or a year . . .

Why do we do this to ourselves? Maybe it's because we have a wrong perception of God. For some, the Lord seems more like an idea than a real person. Or it feels like God lives in a galaxy far, far away and isn't very useful to us here on planet Earth. To some, He seems angry or scary—like the imposing school principal we avoided in the hallway. How many of us struggle to associate God with treasure, satisfaction, and joy?

Zacchaeus had the wrong perception of God too. To him, the Lord was merely a concept taught down at the synagogue, so he followed after a shiny god called money that he could hold in his hands. For a while, it was really useful. Outwardly, Zacchaeus became rich, prominent, and maybe a bit plump around the middle. But inwardly, his soul was poor, lost, and emaciated. I think a desperate inner gnawing sent him up a tree that day to seek after Jesus, to reach for something better.

Sometimes, I picture Zacchaeus looking a little like Danny DeVito. But inwardly, I think he looks a bit like me. In 2008, I learned that Zacchaeus's chains of "having more" were the same as mine. Hard times taught me a hard lesson. I thought the Lord was my treasure, until I had to actually get rid of some. The stock market crashed and we struggled like everyone else. It was a scary time. We downsized substantially, which was a first for me. My whole life had been focused on upsizing, collecting, and acquiring. "Divesting" wasn't a word I used. Ever. Instead, I used words like "let's shop," "add on," and "I want that," way too much. At first, downsizing was painful, but it was so good for me. I had an estate sale. I sold things online. And I ate some humble pie. Eventually, I just started giving things away. My treasures became a burden. I didn't have room for all of them. Downsizing showed me that I collected too much, and I spent too much time doing it. My life was out of balance and I had paid an inward price.

My idea of how my life *had to look* had to go. God wanted to replace my "dream house dream" with a better one. The verse that says, "store up for yourselves treasures in heaven," was one I needed to apply to myself. (Don't you just love those?) Like a heavy, too-short chain, my pursuit of more held me back from seeking God. It wasn't a matter of having things or not having things; it was a matter of where I was putting my focus. Ouch.

For God to become my treasure, I had to let go of some stuff so that I could grasp His hand. As I released my tight hold on things, they stopped having such a hold on me. Looking back, I see that God was working on my heart, just as He did on Zacchaeus's heart. We are controlled by what we treasure most. God wants to free us from the chains that keep us from putting Him first every day. God wants to free us to enjoy Him and to enjoy our lives. He can satisfy us more than "having more" ever can. When we treasure our time with Him more than anything else, then we become truly rich.

Seeking God not only frees us *from* bondage; it also empowers us *to* become different. After spending some time with Jesus, Zacchaeus soon discovered he wanted to change, to get a second chance. Being with Jesus gave him the power to do so. Suddenly Zacchaeus's demeanor changed completely, turning even joyful, almost like he was someone else—a new person. Paul explained this miraculous inner makeover when he wrote: ". . . anyone who belongs to Christ has become a new person. The old life is gone; a new life has begun," (2 Cor. 5:17 NLT). Zacchaeus's change of heart is as miraculous as any healing or sign.

Spending time with Jesus gives us the power to grow and change too. This is why we need to seek and find Him repeatedly. Seeking the Lord changes what we value. When Zacchaeus decided that following Jesus was more important than money and power, he made amends by giving back four times the amount he had taken. That's pretty generous for a crook! But Zacchaeus went even further by giving half of his immense wealth away to the poor. *Half.* Experiencing God's love freed him to change dramatically.

This seismic shift in attitude made me wonder how Zacchaeus lived the rest of his life. What happened to him? Where did he go? Did he continue imitating Christ? I did some research and found that church tradition claims that Zacchaeus eventually accompanied Peter on his missions. He followed Peter to Caesarea, where he served as the first bishop of Caesarea.[1] I'm not sure if this is true, but it seems pretty likely. I imagine Zacchaeus spent the rest of his life enjoying and sharing the boundless riches of Christ with others.

SEEKING FREES US TO CHANGE

Despite my last name—Patterson—I am not Irish or Catholic. Consequently, I never learned much about Saint Patrick when I was growing up. The holiday in March meant lucky four-leaf clovers, wearing green or getting pinched, and specials at local bars. I don't know all of Saint Patrick's beliefs or opinions, but his story is worth sharing.

Strangely, Patrick wasn't even Irish—he was English. He was only a teenager when he was captured by Irish pirates and taken to Ireland as a slave. He was alone and scared, so he began to seek after God. As Patrick tended sheep in the green pastures of Ireland,

he spent the long days enjoying God. While he was a slave,
Patrick found freedom and riches in God.

After six years in captivity, he felt the Lord leading him to
escape. He slipped away one dark night but didn't know where to
go. He found a road and started walking. Eventually, he came to
the coast and found a ship to take him back to England. But after
returning home, Patrick just wasn't the same—his encounter
with God's love made him want a different life. So he studied
to become a missionary. Later, he made the difficult decision to
go back to Ireland and share his faith with people who had no
knowledge of God or His Son, Jesus Christ.

Patrick baptized thousands. He established monasteries and
schools all over Ireland. Irish monks actually are the ones who
were responsible for preserving many of the ancient Bible texts
during the Dark Ages. When Irish immigrants came to America
more than a thousand years later, they brought their Christian
faith and Bibles with them. So in a way, Patrick shared with us
too. He wrote, "All that I am I have received from God. So I
live among barbarous tribes, a stranger and exile for the love of
God."[2] Patrick found freedom in God, and this inspired him to
adjust his priorities and to live differently.

My life experience is not nearly as dramatic as Patrick's;
there are not many ships, pirates, or barbarians in my story.
But seeking after God has changed my life. Part of my journey
includes my downsizing experience and discovering what it
means to value my relationship with God more. This has changed
my other relationships as well. It's given me an entirely new
way to look at life. And it's inspired me to grow, take risks, and
try new things. God used these points in my journey to free me
from bad priorities and to a deeper relationship with Him. His
kingdom has become more important to me than it ever was

before. In fact, my experience of seeking God propelled me toward something I didn't expect.

God uses hard things (like downsizing) for good—I love that about Him. In 2010, my friend, Lauribeth White, asked me to write a retreat curriculum, so I did. And I kept on writing. On a rainy day in 2013, I wrote my first magazine article (oddly, about Saint Patrick). I submitted it on a whim, and it was published. So I began taking writing classes. Freedom from some old things allowed space for something new to happen. My journey has taken me to writing regularly for several magazines and blogging, to speaking engagements, and now to writing a book, which really surprises me! I never dreamed of doing any of this. The more I learn to enjoy seeking God, the more freedom I have to live out my calling and to share my blessings with others.

If we don't make time for seeking God, we will miss the freedom and fulfillment that could be ours. Knowing God has great worth, and it can change anybody. Consider if you are valuing something more than God. Be willing to go out on a limb to find Him like Zacchaeus did. Pray for God to reveal who He is, and to free you from any chains that bind. Ask Him to propel you toward something fulfilling and new. May we all learn from Zacchaeus: seeking the Lord will make us free indeed.

Seek and Find

In Isaiah, God encourages us to seek Him:

Seek the LORD while you can find him.
Call on him now while he is near.
Let the wicked change their ways
and banish the very thought of doing wrong.
Let them turn to the LORD that he may have mercy on them.
Yes, turn to our God, for he will forgive generously.

"My thoughts are nothing like your thoughts," says the LORD.
"And my ways are far beyond anything you could imagine.
For just as the heavens are higher than the earth,
so my ways are higher than your ways
and my thoughts higher than your thoughts"
(Isa. 55:6-13 NLT).

1. In what way do you sense God encouraging you to seek Him more?

2. What do you need most from God in your current circumstances? According to the verses above, what kind of response from God can someone who seeks Him expect?

3. Zacchaeus sought the Lord by climbing a tree. Share about a time when you went out on a limb for God. What was the outcome?

4. Reflect on my downsizing story. What has God asked you to let go? Have you? If not, what is stopping you? What treasures have you received when you have let something go?

5. Discuss or journal about a time when you were freed from a chain that bound you. What new things were you freed to do as a result?

6. When Zacchaeus began giving instead of taking, he impersonated Christ. How do others around you impersonate the King? What kind of impact has this had on you?

CHAPTER 7

David

Seeking Enhances Our Worship

Your procession has come into view, O God—
the procession of my God and King as he goes into the sanctuary.
Singers are in front, musicians behind;
between them are young women playing tambourines.
Praise God, all you people of Israel; praise the Lord, the source
of Israel's life.

PSALM 68:24-26 NLT

The church dutifully sang every verse of "Rock of Ages." The singing wandered a little off-key and the tempo moved even slower than molasses in January. But it definitely wasn't winter; the July day was stifling hot. I was an impatient thirteen-year-old, fidgeting in my seat, frustrated that my parents were making us attend this backward country church while we were on vacation. Our larger, more modern church at home seemed so much better.

As hand-held paper fans with Jesus's picture on them slowly waved back and forth, I began to wonder if the service would ever end. But we were just getting started! A red-faced, white-haired preacher got up and yelled loudly for the next hour. The clock ticked. Sweat ran down my back. The world seemed to stand still. Finally, the last amen was said, and I left thinking, "What a waste of life. I got nothing out of that!"

Most likely, we've all had our share of dry, frustrating, I-got-nothing-out-of-it worship services. Sometimes, our personal worship isn't much better. But seeking God through worship is one of the most powerful ways we can seek Him. So what can we do when we struggle to connect with God? When our worship becomes dull and rote, when the clock is ticking and it feels as if we're being fanned to sleep, how can we enhance it? How can we find more joy and pleasure in it?

We can learn a few things from David. He had some of the most meaningful worship experiences recorded in the Bible. He wrote beautiful descriptions of worship throughout the Psalms. Perhaps exploring one of his best worship experiences will help us learn how to overcome dry worship when it happens.

David Seeks

At dawn, I ride with my men through the hill country, just west of Jerusalem. As we pass by a group of shepherd boys walking behind their sheep, I smile. Not so long ago, I was one of them. Now I am the King of Israel. I've come so far! The journey hasn't been easy. For fifteen years I had to face giants, hide in caves, and fight more battles than I can count. But I've come to understand God's purpose for making me king.

The ark of the covenant has been displaced for years. Without it, tabernacle worship has been disrupted and the people have drifted away. The ark is God's dwelling place among His people, both literally and figuratively. It's time to invite His presence back into our midst. A few months ago, we attempted to bring the ark back to Jerusalem, but we were not successful. Uzzah, one of the attendants, was struck down for failing to show proper respect. Today with great caution and reverence, I hope to bring the ark back to its rightful place, and thus bring my nation back to God.

All morning, people have been busily preparing for a special worship procession. They have traveled miles through pastures, over mountain passes, and across deserts to be here. Singers and band members gather and begin warming up; priests and Levites consecrate themselves with holy water. Thirty thousand people wait expectantly to walk in a grand parade of worshippers behind the ark as it is carried home.

Many seem surprised at my plain appearance as I arrive. I'm dressed simply in white linen, without my royal robes and crown. Today's worship procession is not about my glory—nor will I make it so. The celebration will focus on God's journey home to dwell again among His chosen people. This time the ark will be carried carefully on poles, as prescribed by the Law.

Nervously, the people strain to see the Levites lift the ark and take the first step. The crowd gasps with relief when no one is struck down. The Levites carry the ark five more steps, and everyone cries out for joy because God is with us. The ark is finally coming home!

What great joy it is to worship together in the presence of God! Never before have I seen the people praise Him so passionately. The jubilation God has placed in their hearts fills me with wonder. This is the purpose of my life's unusual journey: reuniting the people with God. And it's happening before my very eyes.

My soul soars as I worship the Lord with my people. I can't help but release my joy with all my might. As we near

Jerusalem, the crowd follows my example, worshipping louder and louder with singing, shouting, and blasts of music. Our joy is contagious; as we near Jerusalem, others join in. We seek and celebrate the Lord as if we had one voice, as if it's our first time to really do so as a nation, and perhaps it is.

As I lead the procession, I find myself leaping and dancing like a child. As I fulfill my God-given destiny, I feel lighter than air, and so near to God. When my wife, Michal, ridicules my unrefined behavior, I reply emphatically, "I *will* celebrate before the Lord." I won't let anything stand in my way.

Bringing the ark back to the tabernacle was probably one of the best worship experiences of David's life—in fact, it's one of the best worship stories recorded in the Bible. Although David was mocked by some, I'm glad he let loose! I can't help but smile as I read about David dancing, in a loin cloth, with his people with all his might. The presence of God filled David with delight, and I love what he wrote about worship on this historic day:

> Glory in his holy name; let the hearts of those who seek the LORD **rejoice**. Look to the LORD and his strength; seek his face always. . . . Let the heavens **rejoice**, let the earth **be glad**; let them say among the nations, 'The LORD reigns!' Let the sea resound, and all that is in it; let the fields **be jubilant**, and everything in them! Let the trees of the forest sing, let them sing **for joy** before the LORD, for he comes to judge the earth. Give thanks to the LORD, for he is good; his love endures forever (1 Chron. 16:10-11, 32-34, emphasis mine).

RECALLING OUR BEST WORSHIP EXPERIENCES

All creation was created to joyfully worship God, like David and his people did. That includes you and I. But let's face it, sometimes worship can feel meaningless and dry. There are days when joyful, exhilarating worship seems impossible. So what can we do to increase our joy and pleasure as we worship God? One way is to recall past worship experiences that caused our hearts to soar.

Like David, many of us have treasured memories of worship: that Easter sunrise service when we felt unusually close to God. The fireside devotional when tears rolled down our cheeks and we didn't care who saw them. That special morning by the shoe rack in our closet when we raised our hands without realizing it. Examining past worship experiences can help us increase our joy in future ones. What made those times so meaningful? How can we recapture that same excitement? Is there something we did then that we aren't doing now?

One of my most memorable worship experiences was at St. Anne's Cathedral in Jerusalem. St. Anne's, an ancient church on the Via Dolorosa, is renowned for its remarkable acoustics. Voices reverberate so beautifully off the stone walls that singing there sounds even better than singing in the shower! (I'll take all the help I can get.)

We arrived at St. Anne's early in the morning, just before the busloads of tourists descended on the old city. Our tour guide asked me to lead our group in a few hymns, so we sang "How Great Is Our God" at the top of our voices under the dome of the cathedral. Suddenly, people coming from a line of tour buses began to flood through the doors and start to sing, as if they were joining a heavenly choir. Much to my surprise, I found myself leading a large assembly in worship, like David did on Mt. Zion.

Not everyone could sing. Not everyone spoke English. It didn't matter. With each verse, the momentum built, and I noticed people crying and holding up their hands. Their faces were illuminated with an inner light. More and more people joined us until the church was packed with Christian pilgrims from across the globe, lifting their voices to God. No one seemed to care about denominational or cultural barriers. Our differences were cast aside that morning for the sole purpose of worshipping our Creator. I've never experienced anything quite like it.

I thought my song-leading-like-David was over when a stern-faced priest in a flowing black robe approached me. After all, I was an uninvited American in a t-shirt holding an impromptu concert in his church. Perhaps we had overstayed our welcome. But instead of saying, "Move on, pilgrim!" he asked me to continue, as if he, too, grasped the beauty and power of the moment. A smile broke out on his face as he said, "Please keep on singing, the people need to worship." So we sang some more.

Finally, a group from Russia asked in broken English if they could sing to us, and they sang a beautiful Russian hymn. Their words were foreign, but their meaning was clear. I saw the light of worship in their faces and heard it in their voices. When they broke out in a Russian version of "Amazing Grace," my tears flowed too.

I imagine David might have felt a bit like I did, as he looked at the crowds dancing, singing, and praising God with all their hearts. I felt like dancing, too, as I watched the joy on faces from all over the world, singing and praising Jesus Christ in the holy city. Maybe it was a bit like heaven will be. This treasured worship memory reminds me of the exhilaration of loosening up and participating, instead of remaining aloof and focusing on our differences. What can you learn from your memories?

PERSONAL WORSHIP COMES FIRST

One way to ensure dry, dull worship is by neglecting to worship
in private, first. I'd much rather blame the church, but I've
learned that dry worship isn't solely their fault (ouch). It's hard
to worship deeply off the cuff. It's challenging to be "on fire for
God" when we come in ice-cold. Personal worship prepares our
hearts for group worship. It's like a spiritual warm up.

My friends Talitha, Carol, and Beth have completed several
marathons. They are very careful to warm up before each event.
Beth explained to me that warming up helps increase blood flow
to the muscles, which results in decreased stiffness, reduces the
risk of injury and, often, improves performance. Some runners
even claim a physical warm up prepares their minds to go the
distance. Worshipping privately before we worship publicly has
similar spiritual benefits: decreased stiffness, less injury (from
others), and improved performance (or engagement).

David spent quite a lot of time worshipping God privately.
He worshipped while he tended sheep in the fields as a boy. He
worshipped in caves and deserts. He wrote about many of these
joyful, satisfying experiences in the Psalms. So when his people
wanted to worship along with him, he was thrilled to share the
experience. No wonder he sang and danced so freely—he had
prepared his heart beforehand. Worshipping God individually
conditions our hearts for group worship too. It can transform
a rotten mood or even help us confront fear. Spending a little
time rejoicing, no matter what, gives us a needed escape from
heartaches and difficulties. Sometimes, we may not feel like
rejoicing. At other times we may feel distracted. But these
feelings don't have to stand in our way. David didn't miss the joy
of deep and fulfilling worship. Let's not miss it, either.

ALL IN THE FAMILY

While worshipping together can multiply our delight, some people feel like they have been there, done that, and moved on. They discard the group experience like an old shoe that no longer fits.

The problem with this line of thinking is that God delights in corporate worship. That is why we are called to do it: "Oh come, let *us* worship and bow down; let *us* kneel before the LORD, *our* Maker! For he is *our* God, and *we* are the people of his pasture, and the sheep of his hand . . ." (Ps. 95:6-7 ESV, emphasis mine). For better or worse, God has placed us in a spiritual family. I often picture Him as the Father ringing the church bell, calling His children to gather at His table. God wants us to celebrate His goodness as a church family, not just on our own.

But many of us have been disillusioned with church— sometimes with good reason. People at church can be hurtful, frustrating, or annoying, so why should we bother with them? We gather for the same reason we gather with our earthly families—because we belong to each other. We share the same blood—Christ's blood. We have the same inheritance. We share a common hope.

God's family get-togethers kind of remind me of my own family get-togethers. Many of my childhood memories of family dinners involve laughter. When my great-grandmother May (whom I'm named after) got really tickled, her top denture would pop out and everyone would erupt with laughter. Thankfully, she laughed too, and our family enjoyed her loose dentures together.

But not all family dinners are brimming with delight. Some are train wrecks. My first official family dinner was a disaster! I made four chicken and wild rice casseroles, a one-dish meal, for the entire family. I didn't know much about cooking, so when the recipe called for a clove of minced garlic, I mistakenly minced an entire *bulb* of garlic for each casserole. Of course, no one could eat it. So, we ended up having bread and water for dinner—and I'm still hearing about it thirty years later!

Family get-togethers include sweet times, funny disasters, and at times, some ugly episodes as well. It's easy to expect the family table to look like a Norman Rockwell painting, but that's not very realistic. Unfortunately, the people closest to us can be the cruelest. All too often, the family table is the stage for angst-ridden drama. Ill will is passed around like the Jell-O. Condescension and guilt are ladled out along with the gravy. Barbs season the main course and are followed by a bittersweet dessert. Sometimes, we may regret getting together at all.

The ugly family-dinner-train-wreck happened to Jesus also. Unfortunately, the Last Supper was not a sweet time of unity or celebration. The night before Jesus was crucified, His mood was heavy and the disciples' bad attitudes only made it worse. They all had selfish agendas. Some were liars. Others were self-righteous. Let's consider how Jesus handled the drama when He broke bread with His spiritual family, just a few hours before His death.

If ever a family get-together should have been idyllic, it should have been this one. It was a historic occasion: the Last Supper and the first Communion. Jesus shares it with friends He loves—those closest to Him on earth. He has shared His heart and mission with this group. He has entrusted precious secrets about the future and the Father to them.

Consider who they were. Evil Judas, the two-faced pretender who had already agreed to sell Jesus out for cash. (I'll bet he was sour company.) James and John used this special occasion to argue about the pecking order. Proud Peter bragged about his rock-solid faith. This tight-knit band of brothers would scatter that very night and leave Jesus alone to die.

Jesus knew all of this before He sat down, yet He chose to commune with a bunch of dysfunctional people. Jesus was exceedingly patient. He didn't let them drive Him away. He didn't throw His hands up in frustration (I would have). Instead, Jesus broke bread with them and stooped low to wash their feet. If Jesus could gather and break bread with these people, shouldn't we be willing to do the same?

Consider the benefits of fellowship:

Two can accomplish more than twice as much as one, for the results can be much better. If one falls, the other pulls him up; but if a man falls when he is alone, he's in trouble.

Also, on a cold night, two under the same blanket gain warmth from each other, but how can one be warm alone? And one standing alone can be attacked and defeated, but two can stand back-to-back and conquer; three is even better, for a triple-braided cord is not easily broken (Ecc. 4:9-12 TLB).

God gave us to each other for a reason. Sometimes our gatherings will be a train wreck, but other times they will be a blessing. Sometimes we may be called to a different family table, but we are never called to go it alone. Solo Christianity is not God's design; it's a family affair. Seeking Him as a family through worship is a way to increase our joy.

GETTING IN THE SPIRIT

In November, I usually drag the red and green plastic bins of Christmas decorations down from the attic with a groan. There's a tree to trim, sugar cookies to bake, and garland to string. The gift-wrapping and Christmas cards await. Outdoor lights are tangled in a heap. I love Christmas, but it's pretty hard to get excited about all the work it requires. So how do I get in the holiday spirit? By engaging my five senses. I turn on my old Carpenter's Christmas CD, light a holiday candle, and put up a few lights. Next, I bake sugar cookies and after sampling a few, I wind up dancing around the kitchen to the music in my apron, using my spoon as a microphone, miraculously enjoying Christmas after all.

It's the same with worship. While I want the exuberant, exciting kind of worship that David had, sometimes I'm just *not dancing*. I know I'm not the only one. When worship feels dry, it may indicate that my physical senses aren't fully engaged. Each part of worship, like music or communion or prayer, is designed by God to stimulate a different sensory area of the brain.

Consider how our sense of sight can help us worship better. Visual symbols like a cross or even the light of a candle can trigger our minds to go deeper, quickly. Watching other worshippers can enhance our own experience too, just like it did for David (and me) in Jerusalem. Perhaps the Bible is filled with visual language, symbols, and word pictures to engage our brain's sense of sight to connect us with the unseen God.

Then there is the sense of smell. Some churches address it by burning incense. This gives worship a memorable aroma, symbolizing the praise rising to God and stimulating our brains in the process.

Our sense of taste is aroused when we take Communion. Kneeling and lifting our hands engages our sense of touch, allowing us to express our worship physically.

Music awakens our sense of hearing and moves our hearts toward God. Some studies suggest that music stimulates more areas of the brain than anything other stimuli. Music quickly triggers our memories, emotions, and thoughts. It's no wonder, then, that God designed worship to be a musical event. We see examples of a variety of songs, individuals, choirs, and instruments throughout the Bible because music moves us in ways we can't explain. Even in heaven right now, God is using music—choirs, harps, and trumpets—to sound out a new song.

Unfortunately, some groups limit the sensory experiences in worship, which can limit participation and enjoyment. God understands how distracted we can get, so He embedded these sensory "triggers" within the worship experience to help us focus on Him quickly. Once we understand this, we can use these triggers to get us into the spirit of worship even when we don't feel like it. This may mean lighting a candle or bowing our heads as we worship alone on the screened porch. It might include adding some kneeling benches at church or strumming a guitar at a devotional. One of my friends puts a tiny drop of lavender oil under her nose every time she worships. The familiar scent stimulates her mind to connect with God quickly.

Consider how engaging your senses might deepen your worship. Rekindle the joy of past experiences. Condition your heart through personal worship. This will help you worship God with your mind, body, and soul, like David did.

SEEING THE BIGGER PICTURE

I failed to get anything out of the lengthy, tired worship service at the beginning of this chapter because I didn't grasp the bigger picture. I limited my worship to that tiny country church on a hot July day. The writer of Hebrews paints a much bigger picture: "But you have come to Mount Zion, to the city of the living God, the heavenly Jerusalem. You have come to thousands upon thousands of angels in joyful assembly, to the church of the firstborn, whose names are written in heaven" (Heb. 12:22-23).

Whether we are worshipping privately or with a group, it's important to realize that we are joining an event already in progress—worship in the spiritual realm. We can be transported, even while sitting in a pew, to join in worship with saints and angels. From our closet, we can travel to the heavenly Jerusalem. Most of us need a little vacation from today's problems. Worship offers us a break. It leads us to another time and place.

I think C. S. Lewis might have been thinking along these lines when he wrote *The Lion, Witch and the Wardrobe*. Once Lucy stepped through the wardrobe, she stepped into an entirely different world or realm. This new realm existed right beside the old one. Both were real places. And Narnia, the new realm, became the place she loved to be more than anywhere else. I like to think of worship as the wardrobe—a door to another place. The spiritual realm exists alongside (or above) our physical world. It is just as real as our world, or even more so. While the spiritual realm represents our future home, it is a place we can go to right now through the door of worship.

It seems like David must have grasped this grand, bigger-than-this-world picture of worship too. Perhaps he sensed that hosts in the spiritual realm worshiped alongside him. Maybe this was the source of his excitement as he and the people worshipped behind the ark. It can serve as a source of excitement for us too.

Each time you worship, whether publicly or privately, dedicate the time to seeking God. Tell Him you are coming to see Him. Anticipate the joy of meeting Him. Engage your five senses. Loosen up and let go. God's people are leaping and singing, even now, in the spiritual realm. Let's join the celebration!

Seek and Find

1. Read Psalms 16:11; 22:22-31; 100 and 150. Do you find it difficult to celebrate or rejoice in worship? Why or why not?

2. Describe your best worship experience. Why was it meaningful?

3. Discuss or journal about how the different parts of worship are designed to trigger sensory experiences for the mind, body, and soul. Which trigger enhances your worship the most? Sight, sound, smell, taste, or touch?

4. Are you disillusioned with group worship? What did you learn about the first Communion that encourages you? Write a prayer asking for the willingness to continue worshipping with God's people.

5. Sin, hardship, and pain may keep us from enjoying worship. Make a list of anything that might be preventing you from celebrating in God's presence. Find and list verses that can help you overcome these obstacles.

6. Study further and discuss the concept of our joining the ongoing worship in the spiritual realm. How does thinking of worship as a door between the two realms encourage you? How does it change your perspective of worship?

CHAPTER 8

Elijah

Seeking Strengthens Our Prayer Life

Our prayers may be awkward. Our attempts may be feeble. But since the power of prayer is in the one who hears it and not in the one who says it, our prayers do make a difference.

MAX LUCADO

Moving our twin freshmen boys into their college dorm rooms felt like we were running in the Olympic races, emotionally. Jumping the hurtles of panic, frustration, sorrow, and joy left us emotionally and physically spent, so my husband, Mike and I indulged ourselves with dessert in our hotel's lobby restaurant late that night. Leaving our boys at Mississippi State was so hard. Were they ready for college? What temptations might come their way? Would they be okay without us?

Betty, the night manager, came by our table and asked us why we were there. She was a large African-American woman with a caring, gentle spirit. She had one of those faces that smiled even when she wasn't trying to. Her dark brown eyes opened wide with concern when she noticed the tears in my eyes. She pulled up a chair, and for some reason, we shared our fears with her.

A big smile broke out across her face as she said, "You ain't the first worried parents. I been there myself." Her eyes seemed to darken even more as she quietly considered what to say. "Listen," she said, "I've learned that the Lord, He got it under control. Trust Him; He got it. It'll be all right. I just know it."

She grew teary as she stood up and wrapped me in a bear hug, lifting me off the ground. She whispered, "The Holy Spirit in my heart told me to come over here and love on you. Yo' job is to pray and then believe in God. That's hard for mamas, but remember, *The Lord, He got it.*"

The hair stood up on the back of my neck. A strange kind of church had just broken out in the Hilton, and we knew we had received a very special blessing. It was more than good advice—it was encouragement from the Lord to trust Him. Betty spoke from His Spirit—familiar words from a stranger's mouth. We went up to our room and got on our knees, thanking God for lifting two weary parents' hearts. We repented for having so little faith that God had heard our prayers. And though that first year of college was really hard, the twins did survive, and we did too.

When Mike and I get frustrated, sometimes we laugh at ourselves and repeat Betty's words to each other. I have even prayed her words back to God as I'm struggling to believe He's got it. The prophet Elijah struggled in prayer too. Although some of his prayers were never clearly answered, he kept on seeking God in prayer anyway. And so should we.

Elijah Seeks

It's hot and cloudless as I travel through the Jezreel Valley. It looks forlorn, as if the Judean desert has come up and greedily taken over. Dry brown leaves and empty fields are on all sides, parched and cracked, as if it will never rain again. The famine has dragged on for years now. Once this was the breadbasket of Israel, the place where the finest crops grew. Now, it sits like a ghostly reminder of what once was.

The parched earth is a physical picture of life without God. Most of the Israelites have forsaken Him. They worship Baal, the favorite god of King Ahab. I don't think many of them understand the connection between water and faith, idolatry and drought. Today, God will connect the dots.

I've called the Israelites to assemble here on Mt. Carmel, along with the prophets of Baal and evil King Ahab, for a demonstration of God's power. I ask the people to make a choice: will they follow the one true God or continue to worship a lifeless idol? I challenge the priests of Baal to call upon their god to send fire to light their altar. The priests aren't successful, even though they pray loudly to their bronze image, shedding blood and tears. Their false god is as dry and useless as the parched valley below. It's starting to dawn on the Israelites that they have put their faith in nothing at all.

Now it's my turn. I stand alone in front of the altar of God, as my servants drench it with water to further demonstrate God's power. The crowd stands silent, straining to hear my prayer: "Answer me, Lord, answer me, so these people will know that you, Lord, are God, and that you are turning their hearts back again."

This one simple prayer is answered with fire from heaven. A supernatural lightning bolt of white-hot flame consumes the entire altar, wet rocks and all. It is a miracle! God demonstrated His great power in response to my simple, one-sentence prayer. The Israelites fall on their faces and worship.

As faith floods back into the hearts of the crowd, I proclaim that the drought is over. I climb higher up the mountain so I can be seen by all, from the first person to the last. I bow low to the ground, reverently kneeling with my head between my knees, and pray for rain.

Nothing happens. Why was my last prayer answered so readily, and now that I have everyone's rapt attention . . . nothing? I put my nose to the ground and pray again, crying out to the Lord for rain. Still nothing.

I send my servant to look toward the sea for clouds—for any sign of a coming answer—yet there is nothing. The people wait anxiously. So do I. Are they surprised at the lack of response? God just answered a prayer powerfully, yet now He does not answer. Have I failed to pray correctly?

After I've prayed seven times in a row, my servant reports seeing only a hint of the coming of rain, but I take it as a sign. I act decisively, telling the king to hurry home so the coming flood will not stop him.

A small cloud forms out of the sea, far against the horizon. And in a little while—not instantly as before, but slowly—God sends rain. And when the rain comes, it pours. The heavens open up and release three years of stored moisture. The drought is finally over! The famine will soon be behind us. I sought God in prayer on this historic day and found Him to be listening.

We might assume that God answered Elijah's prayers because Elijah was a high-ranking prophet. But Elijah had times of weakness and fear. For instance, after the great miracle at Mt. Carmel, Elijah feared for his life. He ran to the wilderness and asked God to basically "just kill me now." God ignored this prayer altogether!

We, too, can feel like our prayers are being ignored. Maybe it's because we have not done many miracles or great works for

God. Or we may wrestle with faith or being faithful. But if Elijah struggled, having to repeat one prayer seven times and having his other prayer ignored, then we should not be surprised that we grapple with prayer also.

LIVING BY FAITH

In our struggles with prayer, our job is to believe that God hears us, even when we don't yet have an answer. Living by faith is learning to say, "The Lord, He got it," or, "I don't understand, Lord, but I'm choosing to trust you anyway." Honestly, I would much rather live by sight than by faith. I want my life mapped out and organized. I like predictable. I like safe. I want life to make sense. Sometimes, I drive myself crazy trying to understand why things happen and how God is working. Maybe you have done that too.

When it seems like God doesn't hear us or flatly says "no," it can make continuing to pray very hard. Elijah's prayer life shows us that prayer is not an exact science. We may not understand the mystery of answered and unanswered prayers, but we don't have to. Like Elijah, we can pray as an act of faith, no matter what God's response may be.

Elijah's prayers at Mt. Carmel contain three powerful aspects that we can apply to our own prayer life: humility, directness, and persistence. Like Elijah, we can diligently seek the Lord in prayer, trusting that He hears us and will respond in His own way.

HUMILITY

A big, burly guy named Hank (a.k.a. "Tank") once commented in a class I was in that kneeling is an ancient Middle Eastern custom that is unnecessary for Americans today. Earlier in his life, Hank was an offensive guard for the Auburn Tigers, until he blew out his knees. Maybe to him, kneeling represented pain. To others, it might seem old fashioned, weird, or unnecessary. Maybe it's this thinking that causes us to leave kneeling benches out of so many of our churches.

I guess kneeling and bowing isn't exactly the American way. We are the home of the brave and we stand proud. But as we come before God in prayer, it is important to remember how low we truly are. Elijah models humility by physically kneeling in prayer with his face to the ground. Humbly, he admits that he is merely a servant and that God is all-powerful (1 Kings 18:36, 42).

Sometimes I think we can be a bit too casual as we pray, like we are talking to a good buddy or a neighbor. In today's culture, we seem to have lost the concepts of honor and respect. In this era of equality, we forget that life still has a pecking order. Just ask any high school teacher or policeman. The idea of honoring those in authority has gone the way of leisure suits and mom jeans—out.

However, unlike dated clothes, honor is not a passing style or custom. While kneeling isn't always practical or commanded, the practice of honor and awe is. Kneeling and bowing in prayer is a physical reminder of our spiritual posture. Mark Batterson said, "The physical posture of kneeling, coupled with a humble heart, is the most powerful position on earth."[1] As we seek God daily, it is effective to seek Him on our knees. Kneeling in prayer is modeled throughout the Bible because it is important and powerful, even for Americans.

Praying humbly also includes being repentant and proclaiming God's power in our prayers. I don't know about you, but admitting my own failures isn't always at the top of my prayer list. How many times have I prayed, "Lord, I've gotta have this!" without fully addressing who He is and admitting who I am? Elijah prayed with reverence saying, "Prove today that you are God in Israel and that I am your servant" (1 Kings 18:36 NLT). Now, that's a better way to pray! Acknowledging who God is and confessing our weaknesses enables us to pray with greater humility and power.

DIRECTNESS

Elijah also prays with directness, saying, "Answer me, Lord, answer me." David often asked God to hurry and even gave Him suggestions! Sometimes I fail to ask directly for what I want. I fall for the old adage: "Be careful what you pray for, God might just give it to you." As if God punishes us for asking for things. But when we look at prayers in the Bible, we see directness coupled with respect. Here are a few examples:

- *"Establish the work of our hands" (Ps. 90:17).* In other words, "Help me to succeed. At work. At home. In relationships. Make my work profitable and significant." Direct prayers often get direct answers.

- *"They have no more wine" (John 2:3).* Mary was very direct in asking Jesus to provide for an ordinary life detail. That day, Jesus answered yes by providing extraordinary wine. Jesus cares about details, like not wasting leftover loaves and fishes. This means we can pray for little things as well as big dreams. Peter said to cast "*all* your cares on him because he cares for you" (1 Pet. 5:7 NET BIBLE, emphasis mine).

- *"Stretch out your hand to heal" (Acts 4:30).* God is the great physician, caring for our minds, bodies, and souls. Although we may ask for complete healing, God may not grant it—it's His option to say no. But it is always right to pray specifically for healing and then leave it in God's hands.

- *"Give me a heart that understands" (1 Kings 3:9 NIRV).*

We don't have true understanding or wisdom apart from God, yet we often fail to ask for it specifically. We can pray for God to give others wisdom and understanding too.

- *"Make a way for me" (Isa. 43:19, my paraphrase).* God can make a way through the wilderness or storm. Many times our prayers for a way out or through are met initially with the answer of peace in the midst of the process. Later on, we can look back and see that God gave us peace first and eventually made a way.

Much of the time we don't really know what to pray for, but we can ask God for anything. There is no limit to what we can ask. God is not a genie in a bottle who restricts us to only three wishes, yet sometimes we may feel like we are asking for too much. Paul assures us that God can "do immeasurably more than all we ask or imagine" (Eph. 3:20). So we should ask for everything that we need, and then some. It's okay. God loves to give, and give abundantly, but He desires that we ask first, just as Elijah did.

PERSISTENCE

For me, the hardest thing about prayer is persistence. I stop way too soon and give up way too easily. When God seems to say no to my prayers, it's hard to wait for what's next. God teaches obedience and humility in times of waiting, but sometimes waiting on God is as much fun as watching turtles race.

A sarcastic police officer in mirrored shades once pulled me over. He handed me an expensive ticket as he smacked his sour apple gum. "You have a real nice day, ma'am," he smirked, as he walked away. *"Mm—mmm,* you must love speed." Oh, how I hate to admit it, but he guessed right! I love the microwave, Instagram, and Snapchat. Whoever invented those conveniences gets it—most of us hate to wait.

God made Elijah wait for an answer while he prayed seven times with his nose to the ground in front of a waiting crowd. He probably got antsy as he prayed over and over. Finally, clouds began to gather *slowly,* and after a while, it rained. God had a reason for this. It showed the people that Elijah himself wasn't the miracle worker. It taught them how to pray to an invisible God with patience and persistence.

Maybe praying for things over and over shows us that *we* aren't the miracle workers either. Persistence builds faith. It points our hearts away from ourselves to a greater and more powerful God. When we have waited awhile and prayed a lot, God often reveals His answers.

GOD'S UNIQUE ANSWERS

When I get frustrated and want to stop praying altogether, it helps me to remember God's past answers. Those memories are sacred and powerful. Some of His answers can be extremely personal. In chapter six, I mentioned the year we downsized. We sold our house, but we had nowhere to move. (I would never suggest doing this.) I can't explain it, but I agreed to sell because I knew God wanted me to. Mike felt the same way, which confirmed it further. I signed the papers with a shaky hand and prayed for help to find another house. We looked and looked. I waited anxiously. Self-doubt and regret began to swirl in my head like mosquitoes in a Florida swamp.

As moving day loomed, my prayers became more desperate: *Where are we going to move, God? What am I doing? Help!* I asked for a nice home for my family with directness: *What about this afternoon, Lord?*

A few days later, I took an evening walk and laid my heart out to God, reminding Him that I had gone far out on the limb of obedience here, and I admitted I was having doubts. As the cicadas chanted, I sank to my knees on the warm pavement and lifted my hands. I asked specifically for a good house for my family, two cats, and dog. I shed some tears and confessed my anxiety, and even though I heard nothing but the summer night sounds, I felt peace. I thanked God for listening. A beautiful orange moon peeked over the mountains, watching me as I walked home.

When I got back, Mike showed me a one-line ad in the newspaper. The ad was for a house I had always admired; it was the first day it had ever been on the market. And the last. In that brief ad I saw a small cloud on my horizon, just like Elijah's servant did. It was a sign that God heard me. The next day, we bought that house and we live there still. Although it is smaller and not as fancy as our other house, it is our family's favorite. God gave us just what we needed, at just the right time.

Some of God's answers are unique. Sometimes, accepting them requires us to have a larger perspective. For instance, we tend to limit His answers to this life, which may not be entirely accurate. Prayers have no expiration date. Each one is remembered. I learned this by witnessing God's unusual answer to my Aunt Mary Ann's prayer.

Bless her heart, young Mary Ann just couldn't sing a lick. Even the tune of "Happy Birthday" gave her trouble. She tried to sing like all the other kids, but somehow, she just couldn't hit the notes. Mary Ann prayed that God would help her learn to sing, but it just didn't happen. Soon, she forgot all about her prayer.

But God remembered. He never forgets. Our sighs and longings are not hidden from Him (Ps. 38:9).

Seventy years later, my Aunt Mary Ann lived her last day with her children gathered by her side. She was wrapped in a bright blue cotton blanket, so weakened from her cancer that it was hard to talk. When she finally summoned the strength to speak, her children listened intently. She said: "I wish I could have sung like your father; it's one of my biggest disappointments. He sang so beautifully. I can even hear him singing now, if I close my eyes and remember, even though he has been gone for a long time. God has promised me that I will be singing in heaven soon. I can't wait."

Maybe it was the heavy medication. Drugs make people say some crazy things. But everything else she said that day made sense. Her children were confused. Even though she had joked about not being able to sing, they had no idea it really bothered her. Of all the things Mary Ann might have said on her deathbed, why did she say that? She must have valued the ability to sing far more than anyone realized.

A few months after Mary Ann died, Bobby, a distant acquaintance of the family, was also suffering with cancer and nearing the end. One afternoon, he had a vivid dream. When he woke up, he told his wife about it. He couldn't get the exquisite scenes and sounds out of his head. He talked about it for days. Finally, his wife decided to share the dream with Mary Ann's children: "I don't want to make you sad, but we need to share something with you. A few days ago, Bobby dreamed about walking toward heaven's gate. He experienced heaven's beauty—a beauty he could see and feel. A clear, pure voice sang out from the gate to welcome him. He was startled when he realized the voice belonged to your mother, Mary Ann. He didn't really know she was such a great singer. He saw her standing at the gate, singing joyfully. Bobby uses the word 'magnificent' to describe the sound of her voice; he can't stop talking about it. It's given him great peace about going there. We hope it gives you peace too."

And it did. Mary Ann's children still tear up thinking about their mother singing in heaven, just as she said she would. They wonder how they will feel when they first hear her magnificent song welcoming *them* to eternity.

Whether we've prayed about something today or seventy years ago, as Mary Ann did, God remembers our prayers. Since some requests are denied and others aren't readily answered, we tend to forget that each prayer is eternal and precious (Rev. 5:8). Not one prayer is wasted. Not one prayer is forgotten.

Sometimes, we can see that God used His silence to teach us about Himself or build our faith. Other times, we may never understand why a prayer isn't answered. We may live our entire lives enduring bad relationships, bad habits or disappointments, with prayers for deliverance met only with silence. But this life is not all there is; it is merely a preface to eternity. I believe Mary Ann received just what she asked for.

Maybe our unmet prayers don't die with us—perhaps they remain so they can be satisfied in eternity. Yet, sometimes I think of unanswered prayers dismally, as if God's answers are limited to this life. I want to gain a larger perspective. When I am tempted to despair, when pain-filled prayers are met only with silence, it helps me to picture Mary Ann singing in heaven. God answered her prayer with a heavenly answer. Her voice is pure. Beautiful. *Magnificent.* She smiles as she sings, as if it is one of the greatest pleasures she has ever known, and perhaps it is.

God has more in store for us than we can ever know. Perhaps our greatest pain now will become the foundation of our greatest joy in the future.

Seek and Find

1. Think back on times when God answered your prayers. Write down as many as you can remember, and use this record of God's faithfulness to encourage you when you're feeling discouraged.

2. Think of the specific ways Elijah approached God in prayer as you read the verses below.

Humbly:

"Come, let us worship and bow down. Let us kneel before the Lord our maker, for he is our God" (Ps. 95:6-7 NLT).

Do you kneel in prayer? What are your thoughts about kneeling and other prayer postures?

Do you regularly confess your sins and failures to God? Even though this isn't easy, it is cleansing and healing to the soul. Take some time today to acknowledge your shortcomings to God.

In what ways do you acknowledge God's power in your prayers? What words of praise could you offer?

Directly:

". . . The earnest prayer of a righteous man has great power and wonderful results. Elijah was as completely human as we are, and yet when he prayed earnestly that no rain would fall, none fell for the next three and a half years! Then he prayed again,

this time that it would rain, and down it poured, and the grass
turned green and the gardens began to grow again"
(Jas. 5:16-18 TLB).

Do you find asking God for specific things difficult?
Why or why not?

What do you want from God right now? Write a prayer in
your journal about these things and date it. Make your prayer
humble, direct, and filled with praise. Add any answers that
may come later in response to this prayer, and date them.

Persistently:
"Pray in the Spirit at all times and on every occasion. Stay alert
and be persistent in your prayers for all believers everywhere"
(Eph. 6:18 NLT).

Recall or discuss a time when the "answer" to your prayers
was silence, or you had to wait for an answer. How did you
handle it? Does Mary Ann's story encourage you or broaden
your perspective of God's answers?

What have you learned from waiting on God?

What can inspire you to keep on praying, even when nothing
seems to happen?

CHAPTER 9

Ruth

Seeking Helps Us Love Others Well

*Love leaves a legacy. How you treated other people, not your
wealth or accomplishments, is the most enduring impact you can
leave on earth.*

RICK WARREN

*"I've never seen anything like it," I said to the Painter. "It is
exquisite, alive—like nothing I've ever seen before."*

*"Yes," He said. "It is unique and rare. Actually, there is
nothing exactly like this painting in all the world."*

*"When I see it," I said, "I can think of only one word. Not
perfection—it's not without cracks and fissures—but splendor."*

*"You have judged correctly," said the Painter. "That is my
purpose in painting. I always paint with the color of splendor,
every time."*

"What is the painting's name?" I asked.

"I call it Mother-in-law and Daughter-in-law," He replied.

*"But it's so beautiful, so filled with hope, why would you call it
that?" I asked.*

"You base your idea on what you've seen before," said the Painter. "I base my idea on what I have done before and can do again."

"What am I missing here?" I asked. "Why can't I see the beauty in that relationship like you can? I cannot see splendor in an in-law relationship at all."

"That is because you only look at the people in the relationship—not the main ingredient," said the Painter.

"What is that?" I asked.

"Me," He said. "When I inhabit a relationship, it gives off a certain splendor. When I piece shattered relationships back together, they have a special richness, a patina that gleams more deeply than it did before. I give relationships life, beauty, and splendor. I care about each one. I care enough to make them better, to create them as works of art, if I am invited in.

I paint with the colors of love, attention, respect, and forgiveness. These colors blend magically—the only word to describe it is splendor. Examine the brushstrokes of my relational masterpieces carefully and you will find my splendor woven within. Each relationship is a work of art when I paint it."

Few relationships depicted in the Bible exude more splendor than the relationship between Ruth and Naomi. Their story reminds me of a beautiful painting that captures the splendor that relationships can have, but only with God's help. Let's examine the "brushstrokes" of their relationship more closely.

Ruth Seeks

I walk up the steep, winding road toward Bethlehem, exhausted. After days of walking, I've finally reached the Promised Land. A tear slowly scores its way through the dust on my cheek as I think about my life. Like the road, it has been mostly an uphill climb, painfully twisting through loss and difficulty.

A bitter tide of death has swept through our family, leaving only destitute widows in its wake. Plague took the life of my father-in-law. A few years later, my husband and his brother died in a tragic accident. These men were the most loving people I've ever known. Losing them was overwhelming to me and my mother-in-law, Naomi. Desperate with grief, I began reaching out to my husband's God.

I didn't know if Almighty God would accept a poor Gentile widow like me. I sought Him anyway; I needed to belong to someone again. Soon, I began to feel God's acceptance and to know His love; it has given me a wondrous sense of comfort that I can't explain. I've come to realize that God placed me in this Jewish family as a way of including me in His kingdom. God had a plan for me even before I believed in Him! I've noticed that the more time I spend with God, the more I change for the better. I've become so filled with His love that it's spilled over to others, cascading down into every relationship I have.

When my mother-in-law decided to return to her home in Bethlehem, I chose to come with her. It's a dangerous trip and Naomi is old, so I left Moab, the only home I've ever known, to walk alongside her. The trip to Israel has taken days. We were utterly alone, a pair of destitute widows clinging to each other, as vulnerable as lambs. Somehow, I found water and shelter when we needed it. Naomi told stories about God along the way.

Now that we have arrived safely in Bethlehem, we seem to be the talk of the town. Everyone is astonished that we crossed the desert by ourselves. The Hebrew women eye me suspiciously. I'm an outsider, a Gentile, the kind of daughter-in-law Naomi must be ashamed to have.

But Naomi isn't ashamed. She praises me all over town, telling our survival story with dramatic flair. Her friends are spellbound as she tells them how I refused to leave her, saying: "Where you go I will go, and where you stay I will stay. Your people will be my people and your God, my God."

We live mostly on handouts from family and friends. At harvest time, I glean the leftover grain in the fields so that we will have enough to eat. As I gather up golden stalks of barley at a nearby farm, I sense God's pleasure.

I've lost just about everything, except for my youth. Boaz, the landowner, walks by and I quickly bow my head—it's improper for a Gentile woman to meet his gaze. Later, he surprises me by introducing himself and asking me to join him for lunch. I accept his kindness, even though I don't understand it.

Naomi is delighted when I tell her about it. She explains that Boaz's mother was Rahab, a courageous Gentile woman who helped the people of God. No wonder he was so nice to me— Boaz understands how an outsider must feel. He appreciates me, not for my pedigree, but for the love I've shown to Naomi and to God. Boaz said: "I have heard how you left your father and mother and your own land to live here among complete strangers. May the Lord, the God of Israel, under whose wings you have come to take refuge, reward you fully for what you have done."

A month later, we get married. Finally, I am no longer considered an outsider. I am home.

It's harvest time once again, and outside the window of my new home, I watch Naomi in wonder. She holds my newborn son, Obed, proudly in her arms, showing him to her friends. I've never seen her face look more joyful. I hear her friends say to her: "May he become famous throughout Israel! He will renew your life and sustain you in your old age. For your daughter-in-law, who loves you and who is better to you than seven sons, has given him birth."

Little did I know how God would bless my son, by making him the father of Jesse, the father of David, and thus establishing him in the lineage of the Savior to come.

God desires to deepen and strengthen the bonds we have here on earth, like He did for Ruth and Naomi. In Luke 10:27, Jesus places our relationship with others right after our relationship with Him. The two are linked. Loving God's children well is a way of seeking and loving Him. Seeking Him repeatedly fills us with His love, and it trickles down (eventually) into every relationship we have.

A MODEL RELATIONSHIP

I love the captivating stories in the Old Testament. As I began studying them more closely, I was surprised (and yes, entertained) by the drama and family dysfunction. From incest to murder to jealousy, biblical stories are often darker and more enthralling than an HBO miniseries. (They kind of make some of our issues seem light!) Thankfully, God doesn't just tell the fluffy stuff in His Word. He tells us about the good and the bad, so we can have realistic expectations of each other.

Oddly, the story of Ruth and Naomi is very different from other stories in the Bible. It models perfection in one of the hardest relationships of all: the in-law relationship. We see no bitter rants, sour grapes, or catfights in the book of Ruth; all we see is love, respect, and syrupy sweetness. If God typically shows us both sides of the relational coin, then why doesn't He do that here? Is God trying to make us feel guilty or quit trying? How can any of us ever have a relationship as flawless as this one?

Perhaps God provides this "relational masterpiece" as an example of what He can do in our lives. Since God is the source of all love (1 John 4:7), He supplies us with love as we seek Him. The more we seek God, the more love we have to give away. We love and care for others on three distinct levels: physically, emotionally, and spiritually. When God's love is generously applied at every level, a masterpiece forms.

PHYSICAL CARE

When we think of family relations, we often think about physical care: bringing home the bacon, laundering smelly clothes, steadying Granny's walker, preparing the Thanksgiving turkey. But in Ruth we see an unusual kind of daughter-in-law—one who actually risks her life by walking through a desert with her mother-in-law. Ah, Ruth was a keeper. She shared a home and worked in the fields just to feed Naomi. Ruth cared for her to the point of physical sacrifice. That's hard to do, but Ruth's example can inspire us to make little sacrifices for those we love, like forgoing a new dress so your daughter can have one, picking up a prescription at midnight for your mother-in-law, or helping your spouse with the dishes or yard work. While we can't meet every need for everyone, it's important to meet the needs that we can, without complaining.

It's amazing to me how Ruth sacrificed without acting like a martyr. In fact, her attitude has put me to shame more than once. I remember a time when I offered to bring soup to a sick relative. The traffic was horrendous, but my attitude was even worse. I sped down the road angrily, kids in tow, feeling overwhelmed. As usual, I had overpromised and overscheduled. The kids had sports practices and, of course, one of them had left a shoe behind. (Who remembers one shoe and forgets the other?!)

We ran by the house, got the shoe, and raced toward practice, but I could go only about twenty miles an hour due to repaving work. I could see and feel the waves of heat rising from the hot asphalt—and from the top of my head. The car in front of me had a bumper sticker that said, "Not enjoying my exhaust? Then back off!" I decided to tail it even closer.

I felt dangerously explosive when I finally arrived (late) to football practice. Once I let my boys out, I sped to deliver dinner. For a crazy moment, I considered tossing the container of soup out of my window toward the front door without stopping. *Why does my family get sick and cause me such trouble?* I still had to get my daughter to dance practice and cook our supper.

I left the car running and ran up to the front door. Breathlessly, I said, "Hope you enjoy it; I've got to run," and practically threw the soup at my relative. She looked a bit wounded but thanked me and asked me to come in and visit. I couldn't, of course, so I said no. In the middle of the night a few weeks later, I remembered that I hadn't even called to check on her, much less visit. I had cared with my hands, but not with my heart.

Ruth's love went deeper than the dutiful check-the-box kind of love, and ours can too. God wants us to seek Him so He can help us love other people the way He loves us.

EMOTIONAL CARE

In many families, a glaring lack of emotional care causes pain and destruction—not a pretty picture. In contrast, Naomi and Ruth's relationship beams with tenderness and joy. That's because they loved each other on a deeper level—the emotional level.

When I was in my early twenties, I really struggled with relationships. I felt distant from friends and colleagues. At times,

I simply lacked the confidence to extend myself and be friendly.
I wasn't sure what I was doing wrong. Years later, in a biblical
counseling class, I discovered this wonderful truth: everyone has
a *set* of similar emotional needs, and when these needs aren't
met, relationships suffer. Learning this really helped me. Like
a bull in an emotional china shop, we can easily trample over
needs and shatter fragile emotions before we know it. I really
don't want to do that, so I compiled a list of essential emotional
needs, based on the story of Ruth and other Scriptures. These
needs must be met in order to foster vibrant, loving relationships.

Acceptance. In Ephesians 4:2-3, Paul encourages believers
to maintain unity. Unfortunately, many mistake uniformity for
unity, but they are not the same thing. In the spirit of uniformity
(and tackiness, sometimes), family members often dress alike
for Christmas card photos. But this emphasis on uniformity can
go way beyond Christmas cards to pushing everyone to have the
same opinions, preferences, and actions.

Practicing acceptance means that we can still have loving
relationships while pulling for different football teams or political
parties, or even going to different churches. None of those
issues are worth sacrificing a relationship for. Sure, there are
some things that are unacceptable, but that list should be very
short and our arms open wide. Consider the lack of uniformity
between Ruth and Naomi: Ruth was an Arab; Naomi was a Jew.
They probably cooked differently. Ruth might have preferred
Moabite fashion. Naomi probably had very different holiday
traditions. Yet, throughout the book of Ruth, these women
looked past their differences and loved each other well.

Gratitude. Ever dread going to a family dinner? Even going
to the gynecologist can seem preferable to making chitchat with
annoying Cousin So-and-So. It's really hard to be grateful for

family members who might be peculiar (or obnoxious).

One year, when I was dreading a Thanksgiving get-together, I decided to make a list of ten good things about each person who would attend the dinner. By the time Thanksgiving rolled around, I was overflowing with love. I bounded into the room actually excited to see everyone again (even Cousin So-and-So). Why? Because I took the time to be grateful. Naomi did, too. She asked the Lord to reward Ruth's kindness (Ruth 1:8). That means she had to spend some time thinking about it.

Often families focus on expectation rather than appreciation. Mom is supposed to cook, clean, and be on call. Wives expect husbands to mow and fix things. Parents expect good grades and good attitudes. Wishing for *how* we want others to be can prevent us from appreciating *who* they are. Increasing appreciation draws us closer.

Encouragement. Naomi encouraged Ruth to "wash, put on perfume, and get dressed in your best clothes" (Ruth 3:3). In other words, Naomi wanted Ruth to glam up and pursue a better life for herself. They shared a dream for Ruth's future.

Sadly, sometimes we conceal our dreams and struggles from our families because relatives can be pretty discouraging. We roll our eyes at our brother who is trying to become a screenwriter. We mock Aunt Carol's singing. We joke about Dad's big nose or Mom's Southern drawl. We *jeer* far more than we *cheer*. The Bible teaches us to treat each other differently: "encourage one another and build each other up" (1 Thess. 5:11). When family members cheer each other on, it results in a deeper connection.

Respect. Once I went to a middle school cheering competition and heard a mom berate her twelve-year-old for missing a jump. The little girl struck back fiercely, shouting, "Shut-up Mom! I hate you." I felt like ducking for cover!

When we are angry, it's easy to talk down, dirty, and hatefully to each other. Sometimes we want respect without giving any. God wants so much more for us than this. Consider the Ten Commandments: the first four commandments tell us how to respect God. The other six tell us how to respect one another. God is pretty serious about respect, both for Himself and others (Exod. 20:1-17). Mutual respect enabled Naomi and Ruth to help each other get through tough circumstances. It can do the same for us.

Blessing. God could have dropped gold coins from the sky or at least sent some camels for Naomi and Ruth's trip. He could have provided bottled water and air conditioning. Instead, God cared for Naomi by providing Ruth. He cared for Ruth by sending Boaz. God most often uses people to bless people.

Becoming a source of blessing apart from God is pretty hard to do. God can make us a *channel* of His blessing to other people, just as He did for Abraham (Gen. 12:2). As we seek Him, He points out opportunities to bless those around us and supplies the love that we need. Author and speaker Kevin Elko once told me: "Don't pray for blessing to come into your life; pray to be a blessing."[1] That's great advice. When we partner with God to become a source of blessing, our relationships flourish.

Forgiveness. My friend "Dan" received a toilet from his mother-in-law for his birthday. Really—I'm not making this up. That was his special gift, just from her. And that pretty much symbolized their relationship—in the toilet. The mother-in-law didn't like how Dan resisted her meddling. Dan was often impatient with her. Fortunately, Dan and his mother-in-law have worked out their earlier game of tug-o-war, and the toilet gift is a favorite family story. This transformation didn't just happen; forgiveness was critical.

While we don't see Ruth and Naomi forgiving each other specifically, I assume they must have forgiven each other often. After all, they were flawed human beings just like we are. Paul wrote to the Ephesians, "Be kind and compassionate to one another, forgiving each other, just as in Christ God forgave you" (Eph. 4:32). Loving relationships require a regular flow of forgiveness in order to work.

Thankfully, God helps us to forgive. He has certainly helped me. God has healed and restored relationships that I thought were ruined forever. These are the most beautiful relationships of all—even more beautiful than before they were broken. Any time we see reconciliation like this, rest assured, it didn't happen on its own. We live in a world filled with hate. When we see the beauty of love and forgiveness, we see the hand of God. He softens hearts and circumstances and enables us to forgive. Family and friends *will* let us down—expect it. Forgiveness maintains relationships through the storms of disappointment.

SPIRITUAL CARE

Talking about God makes some of us uncomfortable, so often we keep our mouths shut. We might passionately disagree with family members on religion, so we avoid sharing or even discussing it. Caring at the spiritual level is most often neglected (at least, by me) because it's just easier. We can stick to safe subjects like football, weather, and kids' activities, but by dodging spiritual conversations, we can easily neglect to love our family members' souls.

Ruth and Naomi weren't guilty of dodging religion. The family shared and cared spiritually so that even Gentile Ruth was welcomed into the family of God. Even if we can't come up with a good way to share or talk about our faith with our loved ones, we can pray for them. Praying is a powerful way to love at the spiritual level.

My friend, Rica McRoy, comes from a Hindu family. Years ago, she became a Christian. Since then, she has prayed fervently for her family members to know Christ. But Rica's mother holds tightly to her Hindu faith. She has even converted a walk-in closet into a meditation room. Every day her mother burns incense, meditates, and prays to her idols. And every day Rica keeps on praying.

God has honored Rica's prayers. Her brother and his family have become Christians, as well as many of her friends. This is a picture of spiritual care—beautiful Rica on her knees, loving her mother, brother, and family in the deepest possible way.

When Rica told me about this, I was stung with the realization that I didn't pray about the spiritual well-being of my extended family members. Since my family is Christian, I took their spiritual growth for granted. Since then, I have prayed regularly for their faith journeys.

Spiritual care also includes tangible assistance. Once Mike asked me to please *not* skip vacuuming our closet anymore because he prays there every morning, on his knees. Honestly, this sort of irritated me at first, but later I realized that keeping the floor clean assists him in seeking God. Our help doesn't have to be something hard or "religious." There are small, practical things (even like vacuuming) that we can do to help make the faith walk of our family members richer.

Or not. Sometimes, I am guilty of *over* assistance—especially when it comes to my grown children. For years, I tried to push theological points down their little throats to get them to see what it took me years to grasp. (Confession: I'm a recovering spiritual nag.) I am now learning to give them spiritual freedom, respecting their church choices, listening to their views, and allowing God to work in them as He sees fit. It is far more effective to ask them how I can specifically pray for them than to tell them what I think they should believe. Occasionally I ask them about their relationships with God and how I can help them on their journeys. I encourage them to keep on seeking. But I do it respectfully because being spiritually pushy only pushes them away from me—and God.

Caring spiritually also means supporting the ministries of family members, if possible. Wetherell Johnson, writer and founder of Bible Study Fellowship International, felt God's call after WWI to be a missionary in China. Her family did not want her to go. She left them sobbing in the rain at the train station. Although they meant well, they made it much harder for her to obey God. As the train pulled away, it took all of her strength not to turn back.

Sadly, I've seen husbands lead large ministries without the help of their wives, and vice-versa. These spouses are off doing their own thing, totally missing the relational blessing of being a spiritual helper to their mate. Supporting and encouraging each other in ministry is loving at the deepest and most satisfying level—the spiritual level.

UNDER THE SHADOW OF HIS WINGS

I've had some pretty painful relationships. You probably have too. To me, that's the worst kind of pain there is. I have failed miserably at times in all areas of care, so I've studied a lot about relationships to see what was missing and why they hurt. In seeking God, I learn more about His design for relationships every day. But God is not like a therapist who only gives us good ideas to try. He doesn't just make some rules for us to follow and then wish us well. God is *with us* in relationships; we don't work them out alone.

If you are struggling with relationships right now, try picturing Ruth and Naomi clinging to each other in the desert, underneath the shadow of God's outstretched wings. Imagine you and your loved ones under His wings too. He bound Ruth and Naomi together and protected them. These women represent us, for we relate under the same shadow of His presence.

God wants to help us love one another. Seek Him. Connect with His power. This will change every relationship you have because it will change you. He can increase your love at every level (1 Thess. 3:12). God desires to paint each one of your relationships with the beauty and splendor of love, just like He did for Ruth and Naomi.

Seek and Find

1. Find three verses about loving one another the way God intends. Paraphrase them, using personal pronouns and specifics, as if they were written just to you. Write these paraphrased verses on index cards and put them on your bulletin board or refrigerator.

2. Name some ways you have provided physical care to others, or they to you. How did these experiences make you feel? Are you appreciative of the physical care you have received in the past?

3. Which item listed in the emotional care section is the most difficult for you? Why? Discuss this section with a friend or group. What emotional needs would you add to the list?

4. Does caring on the spiritual level make you uncomfortable? Why or why not? Discuss or journal about how to love (and how not to love) family members spiritually.

5. Write a prayer asking the Lord to help you love others, beginning with the names of those closest to you. Then make a detailed list of ways you can love these people, on all three levels, in the days and weeks ahead.

CHAPTER 10

Hannah

Seeking Leads to Surrender

When God calls you, it doesn't really matter where or what it is,
you just have to surrender to it.

DEVRY COGHLAN

The dog died just as the den filled with luncheon guests. My
friend Beth noticed Maxine, her sweet little pug, lying mighty
still, like a corpse on her red plaid pillow in the den. Before Beth
could react, a group of laughing women sat down to eat their
lunch right next to Maxine, not even noticing her lifeless body.

Beth didn't know what to do. *I could ruin everyone's appetite*
by removing the dead body, she thought, or *just hope no one will*
notice . . .

Maxine was really old and her death was a mercy, but Beth
never guessed that she would die at the party. How do you remove
a dead dog gracefully? She decided just to leave Maxine alone
until the party was over.

A lady wearing pink suede pumps tripped on the rug and
almost fell on Maxine, catching herself just in time on a nearby

chair. Someone said, "What a good dog, she doesn't mind having company" (no, I guess not). Another group of ladies hovered over Maxine and Beth began to sweat. If someone reached down to pat Maxine, she would probably feel . . . a bit cold.

Anxiously, Beth watched as the women stepped around the dead dog in their colorful stilettos and stylish boots. No one even noticed.

When the meeting was called to order, the ladies sat down—in the den. "Your dog must think we are boring," someone quipped. Beth smiled awkwardly. She hoped for an opportune time to remove Maxine, but it never came.

At first Beth was really sad, but later the awkward situation carried a sort of morbid humor—the kind of uncomfortable humor that sometimes emerges at funerals. Eventually, Beth's guests left and she was able to take care of poor Maxine.

This has to be the most awkward luncheon predicament ever. My friends still laugh about it. It's an amazing story when you think about it, a large room filled with people who are totally oblivious to the dead dog right in front of them. If I had been there, I probably wouldn't have noticed Maxine either.

Sometimes, it's easy not to notice the things we really don't want to see. How often do I fail to grasp what is going on right in front of me? Am I blind to the tears glistening in someone's eyes? Do I listen close enough to hear the pain in another's voice? Am I taking note of subtle clues like a sigh or a despondent expression? Probably not always.

It's comforting to know that God isn't like that. He sees every single one of us. He is aware of our need. In tune with our lives. And well acquainted with our hopes and dreams. In fact, one of the Hebrew names for God is *El Roi*, which means "the God who sees me" (Gen. 16:13). I love that name because it reminds me that God sees me every day. It's important to acknowledge that often, lest we forget.

This brings up some nagging questions, though. If God sees us so clearly, then why does He allow painful things to happen to us? Why is He silent sometimes? Why is He so hard to figure out? How can we seek to know a God whose ways are beyond understanding?

While we can't grasp *why* God does what He does, we can grasp *who* He is. He sees our need. He works for our good. He has a purpose in all He does and a purpose for each life (Ps. 138:8 NLT). Since this is true, it's important to consider how God might use our plans and dreams for His purpose. In fact, He has much greater plans in mind for our lives than we do.

This was the case for a woman named Hannah. She chose to keep on seeking God, even though she didn't understand why He denied her most heartfelt request.

Hannah Seeks

The most beautiful brown eyes I've ever seen look up at me in wonder. As I slowly rock my baby to sleep, my heart beats in cadence with his. Being a mother is all I've ever wanted. Surely this is the thing God put me on earth to do. Suddenly, my baby disappears and I wake up screaming into the night. Painfully, I realize it was a nightmare, or rather, that I'm living in one.

Why can't I have children? For seven long years, I've prayed for a child, and yet, God is silent. Each year my heart grows heavier, pulling me down into the dark, chilly chasm of desperation. Trying to understand *why* fills me with confusion; anxiety controls my days and fear stalks me at night. I just cannot bear being barren.

As if my life isn't hard enough, our family is traveling to

Shiloh today to attend the annual feast. I have nothing to celebrate. Peninnah, my husband's younger wife, comes with us. She eyes me with a triumphant smirk as she cradles her newborn baby. My dangling arms throb with emptiness.

Lovingly, my husband places a double portion of meat on my plate at the feast. This only highlights my misfortune. Everyone looks at me in pity, as if I am a cripple. Peninnah spitefully whispers, "Eat up Hannah, I hear roasted lamb gives you, um— *extra vigor.*" Several women snicker. I can't take it anymore, so I excuse myself and run to the tabernacle to seek the Lord.

As I enter, I notice an old woman wearing the dirty, ragged clothes of a beggar. Her wiry hair is shamefully unkempt and her wrinkled face bears an ugly scar. She lays her crutch down and kneels beside it. A glowing, contented smile slowly spreads across her weathered face as she prays. Somehow, she lays her glaring needs aside, along with her crutch, and worships in peace and joy.

When have I *ever* worshipped like that? My every thought centers on what I want so desperately—on how my life should be. I have no room for anything else—my husband, my friends, or even my God. I realize that I've been acting like a victim, refusing to eat, or sleep, or to enjoy living. I can't go on like this, so I pray, "Forgive my lack of faith. Help me accept my life as it is. Forgive me for punishing myself and everybody else for things I can't control."

As I pour out my heart, a new thought, a whispering question, brushes past me like a faint breeze: *How could God use my desire to be a mother for a higher purpose?* I haven't really thought of this before. I always pray for what *I* want, but not for what God might want *for* me. How could God possibly use my dream of motherhood for His great purpose? I can only think of one way.

So I pray an unusual prayer: "Oh God, even though I don't

understand your will, I know you have a purpose in all that you do. Help me surrender my plan to your plan. If you give me a son, I will dedicate him to your kingdom for all his life. Let your purpose for him become my purpose for him."

Eli, the portly High Priest, notices me moving my lips as I pray (an old habit), and he assumes I'm drunk. Piously, he strides over saying, "Put away your wine, woman! This is the house of God." Eli seems uncomfortable when he realizes he's misjudged me. But instead of apologizing, he blesses me, saying, "May God grant your prayer."

When I leave, I leave the grief of trying to understand why behind. Who can decipher God's ways? I eat heartily, enjoying my food for the first time in days. My face is no longer downcast, as I realize I can choose to accept whatever God has for me. Focusing on pain is a killer; I have to start living again. Every morning I lift my hands in surrender praying, "Let your purpose become mine."

As I wake up, the room seems to spin and I run outside and throw up. Uneasily, I sit on a bench, wondering why I feel so queasy . . . and then I laugh in awe. I *will* have a son! I think I'll call him Samuel, which means "heard of God," because God heard me. When I finally let go of my plans and embraced His, everything changed.

Hannah was true to her promise. Embracing God's plan enabled her to give Samuel back to God, even when he was a very young boy. She took Samuel to Eli to serve in the tabernacle as a tiny priest. As she left, she said: "My heart rejoices in the LORD" (1 Sam. 2:1). What a picture of true surrender! Aligning her desire for a son with God's purpose produced *inexplicable*

peace and joy. And it blessed an entire nation: Samuel became a great prophet and ruler over Israel. In addition to the privilege of being Samuel's mother, Hannah had five more children. God had a much greater purpose for Hannah's life than she could have ever imagined.

ACCEPTING GOD'S WILL

When our dreams, prayers, and plans go unrealized, it can be devastating. If we allow it, the disappointment can invade every part of our lives. Although we can't choose our circumstances, we can choose how we react to them. How I *wish* I had known that years ago when I had fertility issues of my own. I can relate to the engulfing desperation Hannah must have felt as she longed for a child. Maybe you can too.

I remember seeing my doctor's eyes narrow as she performed a routine ultrasound. She and the nurse exchanged multiple glances. They measured something about ten times. Then I returned to the examination room, sat on the uncomfortable crinkly white paper, and waited for the bad news. The room smelled like Clorox; it felt as cold and as sterile as I did.

"Fertility treatments will have to stop for at least six months to a year," my doctor said. "You have a large ovarian cyst that may rupture if we continue." Adding another year or more seemed like forever. I don't remember walking out of the doctor's office. I wandered through the steamy parking lot in a daze. I just didn't understand. I had always wanted children, and so had Mike. That was our prayer. Why would God deny it? I couldn't wait another year (or more) to be a mother. I should've already been one.

Going back to work that afternoon seemed like a horrible way-too-heavy burden—so did breathing. My spiritual life was not very strong, and I felt as far away from God as I did from being a mother. If God loved me, why would He not give me a child? I felt like God didn't even notice me or listen to my prayers. Why did I even bother to pray?

As we walked that evening, Mike told me I had to accept where we were. It might take years to have children, or we may never have them. I wanted to fight against this harsh reality with all my heart—as if that would change it. I saw that acceptance was a decision I was refusing to make. That night, for some reason, I decided to accept it.

A month later, I was shocked to find out that I was already pregnant. This *was* God's will for us, after all! It's funny how we never question God's will until it conflicts with our own.

Even though I was so thankful, I didn't spend much time thinking of how I might dedicate my child to God. Unlike Hannah, I didn't stop to consider how He might use me as a mother or use our home for a greater purpose. Instead, I thought about decorating the nursery, maternity shopping, and all the things I wanted next. Isn't that human nature? To get one thing and instantly grab for another? And in doing so, we forfeit our peace.

Surrendering our dreams and plans to God is painful because it usually means we have to change some things. In fact, changing my idea of what my life should be like is one of the hardest things I've ever had to do. Usually, I have a pretty good plan in mind (so I think). And even though God has given me a lot of practice, I still struggle to align my will with His, and probably always will.

For instance, my will is to have a charmed writing career: no deadlines, no dry spells, and no rejections. His will is to grow me through the struggle. I want my children's lives to be super-easy and filled with fun. He wants to build my children's strength and character. I want to say yes to everything and do everything. He wants me to be still. God's agenda always centers on maturing me so I can serve others. Mine usually doesn't. And there's the rub.

Accepting our circumstances and aligning our will to God's purpose is a battle—both inwardly and outwardly. Sometimes, as we are struggling to accept God's will, a "Peninnah" will emerge to ridicule us. At other times, an "Eli" may hang around to misjudge our motives and decisions (can someone say amen?). The evil one wants to keep us bound to a meaningless life, so he often uses others to work against our progress. But if we keep on seeking God, He will help us work past the obstacles, so that we may have the meaningful life He wants us to have.

THE VALUE OF SURRENDER

The most important thing about surrendering to God's will is that it has extraordinary, immeasurable value. I've learned this from my friends, Curtis and Devry Coghlan. When I am struggling to accept God's will for my life, remembering their story encourages me to yield.

Devry Coghlan was abandoned and then adopted later in life. Her painful past inspired her to become a licensed counselor who often worked with orphans. Her husband, Curtis, was a successful journalist. They bought a pretty house on a cozy street and had two precious girls. They went to the neighborhood church and loved it so much that Devry joined their staff as a discipleship coordinator. Devry told me:

For the first time I could remember, my life seemed idyllic. I had a long period of peace and comfort.

When Curtis felt God's call to move to Africa to work with Kenya Relief (a Christian relief organization), I struggled. I had never even been to Africa before. Why would we leave, just

when our life was going so well? I told Curtis I would pray
about it. Over the next few months, I started to sense it was
God's will for us to go. Things I usually enjoyed somehow
seemed to fall a bit flat.

Devry and Curtis finally decided to yield to God's leading.
"It seemed like we were giving up everything—our house, our
cars, our friends—*everything*," Devry said. "What is so amazing
is the abundance that we feel now," added Curtis. "To see the
lame walk and the blind see is one of the greatest gifts you can
receive. Doctors from the U.S. provide excellent care at our
clinic to those who desperately need it. Abandoned children have
a home in our orphanage. I can't tell you what it means to me—
and we could have missed this blessing. Any sacrifice we've had
to make is well worth it."

I began to wonder how willing I am to surrender to God's
purpose for my life. What if God asks too much of me? What if
I am not happy with His plan? Am I willing to follow God even
when I don't know where He is going?

As I talked with Curtis and Devry, I learned how valuable
their surrendering to God's will has been. Last year, Devry found
three abandoned children who were sick and dying in their mud
hut. Christine, the oldest, had advanced conjunctivitis in both
eyes. Each day, her eyesight became more filmy and dim. Her
younger brother, Enoch, had a burgeoning mass on his sternum
and a growing, infectious sore on his back. Their baby brother,
Elvis, had an advanced case of malaria. The hut had no running
water, no food, not even a blanket.

"There are some sights that never leave your mind," Devry
said. "The sight of their squalid home is one of those for me."
Tears ran down her cheeks as she described how desperate the

children were. She had no authorization to take them with her back to the Kenya Relief compound—except that of love and mercy. She put the kids in her van and headed out.

When the three children arrived, an eye surgeon "just happened" to be operating at the clinic that day. She saved Christine's sight. A week later, a visiting pediatric surgeon removed Enoch's mass and cleansed his infected wound. Elvis received treatment for malaria—a $5.00 life-saving remedy that many Kenyans cannot afford. "The children are thriving now," Devry said. "The physical care we give them is wonderful, but the best thing you or I can do for anyone—in Kenya or anywhere—is to share a saving knowledge of Jesus Christ with them. Christine, Enoch, and Elvis, are receiving the greatest gift of all."[1]

I wrote about their story before I knew the three children's names, so as a temporary measure to help me write, I used my own three children's names. This *cut* me to the heart. Tears fell on my keyboard as I typed; suddenly the enormous value of surrendering to God's plan had new meaning. There are lives and souls at stake. There are people whom God wants to reach through you and me. He wants to use our lives to give hope to the hopeless. He wants to save others through us. God only asks us to bend our will to His so that He can do far more than we can ask or imagine.

The Coghlan's story encourages me to surrender to God's Spirit, wherever it leads. It's the most meaningful way to live. My prayer is that it will encourage you too. We only have one life, and even though we may struggle to understand God's ways, we can still seek and find Him. Accepting His path helps us find the peace and purpose that Hannah found. Spending time with God enables us to receive the abundant life Jesus died to give us. It helps us live for something much greater than ourselves—His glorious purpose.

Seek and Find

1. Another woman we're told about in Scripture is Hagar, who didn't realize that God saw her until He spoke to her. Read her story in Genesis 16. Have there been times in your life when you felt like God overlooked you? How did you handle it?

2. "We can rejoice, too, when we run into problems and trials, for we know that they are good for us—they help us learn to be patient. And patience develops strength of character in us and helps us trust God more each time we use it until finally our hope and faith are strong and steady. Then, when that happens, we are able to hold our heads high no matter what happens and know that all is well, for we know how dearly God loves us, and we feel this warm love everywhere within us because God has given us the Holy Spirit to fill our hearts with his love" (Rom. 5:3-5 TLB).

Why does Paul say that hardship is good for us? How has God been El Roi (the God who sees) to you? What trials and problems in the past can you rejoice about now?

3. What circumstances are you struggling to accept right now? Write a prayer asking God to help you surrender to your life as it is, using words and phrases from the passage above.

4. How does Curtis and Devry Coghlan's story make you feel? (Awed? Glad? Challenged?) Do you have any stories of surrender of your own? Discuss or brainstorm with a group about how you could surrender your plans and dreams to God's purpose. What might result?

5. Find several Bible verses about surrendering to God's will and accepting our circumstances. Write down whatever you feel God is saying to you.

6. Read the following description of surrender out loud and discuss it with a friend or group.

Surrender Is . . .
Surrender is accepting life as it is,
instead of how I want it to be.
Surrender is following God,
even when I don't know where He's going.
Surrender is waiting patiently for God,
even when I don't understand.
Surrender is trusting that God will work to bring good out of
each circumstance.
Surrender is maintaining my peace,
no matter what happens.[2]

Commit to reading this often. Note how your experience of surrendering to God's greater purpose changes over time as you seek Him.

CHAPTER 11

Barnabas

Seeking Helps Us Discover Our Gifts

Potential is God's gift to us;
what we do with it is our gift back to God.

MARK BATTERSON

Derek Redmond was at the peak of his athletic career. As he took his place at the starting blocks of the four hundred meter race in the 1992 Olympics, he felt strong. He had suffered through eight surgeries, extensive rehabilitation, and rigorous training to be able to compete. The starting gun fired. Derek had an excellent start but just as he was hitting his stride around the first turn, he heard a loud popping noise. He thought he had been shot. He fell to the ground in excruciating pain with a ruptured hamstring.

As he watched the other runners race toward the finish line, Derek decided to get up and attempt to complete the race. Agony spread across his face as he hopped along, holding the back of his leg, determined to make it to the finish line. He had a long way to go. Suddenly, a man from the crowd ran past the security guards and on to the track. When Derek saw him, he began to sob. Jim Redmond, Derek's father, put his arm around his son and they began walking together. Although doctors and Olympic officials tried to get them to stop, Derek and his dad kept going. Jim kept encouraging him saying, "You are a champion. You are a champion."[1] Derek leaned against his father, and together, they hobbled over the finish line.

There wasn't a dry eye in the crowd. No one really noticed who won the race. Everyone was focused on Derek and his father. When they finally finished, the crowd erupted with cheers and a standing ovation. It's one of the greatest stories in Olympic history. When someone lends his or her strength to another, it is beautiful.

Coming alongside those who are struggling glorifies God. In fact, this is the reason God gives us gifts. Extending our strengths, talents, or encouragement to people who need it is satisfying. It draws us nearer to God and fulfills our purpose. As we seek Him, gifts—in the form of talents and resources—seem to emerge, as if God is inviting us to partner with Him. Consider how a man nicknamed Barnabas found this to be true.

Barnabas Seeks

The wind fills the white sails, pulling the ship forward at a fast clip. Standing at the bow with my hair flying, I smile in wonder. In a way, I am like the ship. Ever since I met Jesus Christ, a wind-like force has pulled my life along. I have no idea where the wind will take me, but I've learned to trust it.

I didn't start out living this way. I was reared as a Pharisee on the Isle of Cyprus. From the time I was born, my life was mapped out for me. My parents sent me to Jerusalem as a teenager to be educated at a proper Pharisaic school. Since I'm a Levite, I continued on in Jerusalem after my schooling, to serve in the temple. I met Jesus there, and just like a ship, my life completely changed course.

When the Pharisees discovered that I was a disciple of Jesus, they cast me out of the temple. This brought an abrupt end to my Levitical role, but my life of service was actually just beginning. After Jesus died, I continued serving His disciples. In those painful days, I discovered that I was a gifted encourager. This was pretty ironic because back in Cyprus, when I was very young, I was often teased about being oblivious to everyone and everything around me. Some called me an introvert. Others called me self-centered. They were probably right. But now, as I seek God, serving others seems to come naturally to me. My given name is Joseph, but the apostles nicknamed me the "son of encouragement," or Barnabas, and it stuck.

The number of disciples grew rapidly in the early days, from a handful of people to thousands. Day and night, I worked to help Jesus's followers. When they needed money, I donated my property. When they needed a teacher, I taught. Soon, I became their trusted advisor. Through serving others, I drew ever closer to the Lord.

Across the world, many souls have come to Christ. Even Saul, the Pharisaic zealot, became a Christian. Before long, Saul began teaching others with fiery words and impassioned rhetoric. That's the way Saul does everything—radically. When Saul came to Jerusalem, I took him under my wing. Endorsing Saul, who now goes by the name Paul, was the right thing to do. Paul, once a strict Pharisee, is teaching Gentiles with me now. Our parents would be dismayed that their straight-laced, respectable Jewish sons are ministering to pagans. God has a remarkable sense of humor!

Initially, I was sent to Antioch to investigate the practices of their Gentile church. These believers were pretty unorthodox, but

I loved them. I was delighted to see the grace of God in them, and I encouraged them all to remain true to the Lord. Realizing that this church was struggling, I went to Tarsus to recruit my old friend, Paul. Together, we've ministered to the believers at Antioch for over a year. Now, we're traveling by ship to preach the gospel to Gentiles in faraway places across the sea. I watch the wind fill the white sails, pulling the boat forward at a fast clip. And I smile. I have no idea where the wind will take me, but I've learned to trust it.

Barnabas went by his nickname; so do a lot of people I know. My cousins nickname everyone—especially people they like. Maybe this is just part of Southern culture or my own quirky circle, I'm not sure, but I grew up using nicknames. Nicknames often describe someone's special talent or place in a group (good or bad). We call one of my friends "Ghost" because he seems to magically appear all over town. Another friend is sometimes called "Anvil" because he is so strong. I even know of a man nicknamed "Toot" (I'll let you interpret that one). Fortunately, Joseph was blessed with a good nickname—Barnabas, or "son of encouragement." This describes how he served: noticing people, coming alongside them, and cheering them on.

I think encouragement is a lost art nowadays—a neglected ministry put up on a dusty church shelf labeled "unimportant." Maybe it's because encouraging is easy to do but hard to track, and even harder to organize. When my friend, Willena Steele, was eighty years old, she discovered that encouragement was her greatest spiritual gift (I guess we're never too old). Since then, she has embraced it as her personal, God-given mission. Willena's blue eyes dance as she greets people at the church door. She will faithfully pray for you, if you ask her to. She often smiles, points her finger at me and says, "Don't you dare give up on that book." And I'm not the only one she encourages. She is so uplifting that some people even call her "little Barnabas" (kind of a nickname of a nickname). Every church needs somebody like that.

People like Willena and Barnabas are rare. While encouragement and coming alongside others is often free and simple to do, we don't always do it. Some of us tend to compete rather than compliment. Others simply don't take the time to notice the needs around them. While cheering someone on can seem trivial, it's important to do because discouragement is everywhere. It usually lurks in hurtful places: among family, churches, and close friends. There were times Barnabas must have felt discouraged, overly busy, or possibly even a bit competitive, but he didn't let these things stop him from coming alongside and encouraging others. And neither should we.

IDENTIFYING OUR GIFTS

The more we seek God, the more we discover about ourselves. In His presence, hidden gifts seem to bubble up from the depths of our soul. Opportunities to develop our talents are revealed. New uses for our resources come to light. Few things can bring us closer to God than following His call on our gifts. And when we use all that we have to glorify Him, it draws us even closer.

Sometimes we cop out by believing we don't have any gifts to use. But each of us does. Peter said: "God has given each of you a gift from his great variety of spiritual gifts. Use them well to serve one another" (1 Pet. 4:10 NLT). If you don't know what your gifts are yet, keep seeking God. He will show you. Seeking God helps us reach our full potential and advance His kingdom. This was certainly the case for Barnabas. God used him in ways he could not have imagined. God can use us mightily, too, when we offer Him our gifts—including both our talents and resources.

One of the best ways to identify our talents is to consider what we love. Often, what we love is linked to our talents. For instance, I love to travel; discovering what God has created fascinates me. Seeing other people and cultures speaks to me. But how can God use that? In many of my lectures and writing, I use examples from my travels to illustrate truth; exotic, faraway places paint memorable pictures in people's minds. Maybe you've noticed the travel stories and examples I've used in this book. My love of travel is connected to my talent of communication. Discovering what we love leads us to our talents.

I have a friend who loves antique buttons—I think that's kind of quirky. She goes to craft fairs and antique markets to find handmade buttons, and then uses them to decorate beautiful picture frames. She gives them to people who need encouragement. Actually, that's not so quirky—it's creative. Her love of buttons links to her talent for art. She uses what she loves to serve others and ultimately, to serve God.

Sometimes, it helps to determine what we don't love. For instance, I hate sewing. I learned that in seventh grade. Every minute of Mrs. Cotton's sewing class (bless her soul) was torture. The carrot-orange pillowcase I made was the ugliest in the class: it was lopsided and too narrow for the pillow. I learned, by sewing, that I have no aptitude or love for sewing. The other day someone asked me to join a sewing group. When I told my friends about it, they howled with laughter. They know that sewing is not my gift, and so do I.

Another time, I remember being thrilled to come down with strep throat while I was volunteering at Vacation Bible School—

no kidding. I would rather have been sick than work my shift. This revealed to me that VBS (especially the crafty part) was not my calling. It was merely grunt work. Sometimes filling in wherever you're needed is necessary, but for the most part we should try minister in places we love and in areas we are gifted for.

My husband was a walk-on football player at the University of Kentucky. He loves everything about football—the camaraderie, the road trips, and even the stadium lights on a crisp autumn night. Now, Mike volunteers as a coach every weekend in the fall. Being on the field with a whistle makes him happy. But I've seen God use football as Mike's personal platform for ministry as well. It's an opportunity to be a good influence and to mentor boys at a formative time in their lives. Mike's love for football links to his talent for mentoring.

Our gifts consist of more than just our talents—they include our personal resources also. Sometimes, our resources can be more useful than our talents. Resources include things we own, our education, training, and past experiences. Barnabas used his resources well: he sold his land to support the church. Most likely, he relied on his religious education as he ministered. He used his personal connections, such as his connection to Paul, to help him serve others. Who could you partner with? How has God prepared you to serve? What do you own that you could share? It's important to consider our resources prayerfully—otherwise we may not think to use them.

My friends Jesse May and Garrett Martz bought a hunting place a few years ago in Alabama's beautiful Paint Rock Valley. As they sought God, they felt led to use their land for others. They kept praying about it, and eventually an opportunity arose. Their property is now used as a retreat facility for Outback America weekends—an exceptional Christian retreat for husbands and wives, parents and teens.[2] I know couples who have torn up their divorce papers because of the healing they received there. I've seen teenagers baptized in the river and others go into ministry after spending the weekend at their hunting place, which is now aptly named the Promised Land.

CONNECTING OUR GIFTS

Interestingly, when we identify and use our gifts for God, He often multiplies them. Jesus said, "To those who use well what they have been given, even more will be given, and they will have an abundance. But from those who do nothing, even what little they have will be taken away" (Matt. 25:29). So according to Jesus, failing to use our gifts results in losing them, but using them increases them.

Sometimes this increase in gifts forms a pattern. Some refer to this pattern of connected gifts as a calling. As Christians, our ultimate calling is to glorify God, but how we do that is very personal. Each calling is as unique as we are. Examining the connections between our talents, resources, and opportunities helps us discover our purpose.

The other day, I found a massive beaver dam. It was an incredible building project! Some busy beaver built an amazing home on his own private lake. It must have taken a long time—lots of effort and thought must have gone into it. I wonder if he enjoyed building it. By the look of it, I think he must have.

Notice the beaver's natural "gifts." They might seem like a random, mismatched set if you didn't know a beaver's calling. But his gifts form a pattern to enable a purpose. They complement each other. While his large, pointed front teeth aren't very photogenic, they are useful for building dams without a saw. His five-fingered hands help him waterproof dams with mud. He uses his flat, leathery tail to smack the water to scare away predators that might threaten construction. To the beaver, it seems like everyone would want to build a dam and live on the lake. What could possibly be better? His busy life is fulfilling, and he becomes skilled by using his gifts to live out his purpose each day.

Like the beaver, we all have natural gifts that can be combined for a greater purpose. Are there connections between the things God has given you? Could they possibly enable a singular purpose? How could you combine them to come alongside another person? Answering these questions leads us to our calling or ministry.

My friend, Art Leslie, grew up in a rough part of town. He went to college on a football scholarship and earned a degree that enabled him to eventually become an executive. Later in life, he lost his job and his marriage. He didn't know what to do. In desperation, he began seeking God like never before. One night, Art came across this verse: "Seek the Kingdom of God above all else, and live righteously, and he will give you everything you need" (Matt. 6:33 NLT). Art felt like God was saying, *Take care of my business and I'll take care of yours.* He sensed God calling him to help kids in tough neighborhoods like the one he grew up in, so he began an after-school program in the projects. This program has continued to grow, adding more children and volunteers each year.

The Huntsville Inner City Learning Center now offers year-round programs that provide biblical teaching, mentoring, tutoring, and fitness training. The center has served hundreds of children and their families.[3] Art's talents include his athleticism, love for kids, and dynamic personality. His resources include his background, education, and work experience. His gifts form a complementary set. Every day, he uses what God gave him to follow his calling.

Usually our calling involves the thing or things we just can't *not* do. It's our special knack or fascination that lingers. Paul wrote, "Each person is given something to do that shows who God is" (1 Cor. 12:7 MSG). In other words, God gives gifts on purpose. Are you using what you've been given to reveal who God is? Dedicating our gifts to a spiritual purpose helps us unravel the mystery and beauty of our personal calling.

USING OUR GIFTS

Sometimes, it's easy to get so focused on our own needs that we fail to come alongside to help others. Just like mules with blinders, we can pass right by people whom God designed us to help. And we miss playing the role we were made to play. As we seek God, He often points out the needs of others to us, like He did for Barnabas. When God reveals a need, He is inviting us to use our gifts to meet it.

Years ago, God revealed my grandmother's need to an Army colonel. Thankfully, he used his gifts of compassion and a sharp mind, along with his authority, to help her on an unbearable day.

In 1942, my grandmother sat on a bench sobbing helplessly in the Houston, Texas, train station. Her heart was broken. She didn't know what to do. And even though the station was filled with people, no one seemed to notice her at all.

Two years earlier, my grandfather had been sent to Alaska, along with his National Guard unit, to build military infrastructure before the outbreak of WWII. His deployment was really hard for her. She had to parent their two young children alone. Their family farm (now known as Jones Valley) became her sole responsibility, even though she had no farming experience. Christmases and birthdays came and went without him. The children barely remembered him. Mail and telegrams had to do, but they didn't, really. Her heart ached to see him again, but as the war raged on, she wondered if she ever would.

One day she received a telegram from my grandfather, asking her to come meet him in San Diego. They could live there for two months while he was on special assignment. She was elated! She hadn't seen his face or heard his voice in two long years. This was what she had prayed for. It was as if God knew she couldn't bear being without him another day.

She and the kids boarded the train excitedly and headed west. The long hours went by slowly, mile after mile. As she talked about the war with other soldiers on the train, she began to realize that my grandfather's special assignment might also be a dangerous one (which it was). She trembled as she recognized that this might be the last time she would ever see him. She couldn't get to San Diego fast enough.

They stopped in Houston to change trains. Her ticket was booked all the way to San Diego, but the conductor wouldn't let her on board. The military had conscripted her train to move troops to the West Coast. She tried to buy another ticket but was told there wouldn't be a civilian train leaving Houston for days. She tried to charm—and then outright beg—the conductor, but he wouldn't let her and the children on the train.

She had no way to get to California. (This was before the days of rental cars and commercial flights.) She was stranded in the train station with two little ones and few options. The disappointment of going so far, and yet not getting to see him, was more than she could bear. Dizzily, she sat down on a bench and cried. The stored-up tears of two long years poured out. She could choke them back no longer. She sobbed giant gasping sobs into her lace handkerchief while the children stared.

Throngs of busy people passed her by. No one seemed to notice her at all, except for one man. A colonel came over and put a gentle hand on her shoulder. Through her tears, she looked up past her wide hat brim and saw his kind face smiling down at her. His shock of white hair gave him a distinguished fatherly air; he seemed almost familiar. He asked her why she was crying. After listening to her story, he was determined to help her get on the train.

The colonel argued with the conductor, but the conductor said, "I can't do it! I've been ordered to fill all westbound trains with servicemen. The lady stays here." But the colonel wouldn't give up. With an authoritative voice, he said, "If this train is filled with men, then the women's restroom will be vacant. This woman and her children will ride in there."[4] And they did. She laid her big brown suitcase flat on the bathroom floor and they huddled on it, resting their heads against the sinks, all the way to California.

My grandfather met them with open arms. The children got to know their daddy again. They rented an apartment near the beach and spent the late afternoons swimming in the blue Pacific. It was one of the happiest times they ever had.

After they got settled, my grandmother desperately tried to find the colonel who helped her. Earlier, he had disappeared into the crowd before she could thank him. Although she had his name and rank, she never could find an address or any record of his existence. But what he did mattered—probably more than he ever knew. This visit gave my grandparents the strength to get through one of the most difficult times of their lives. After leaving San Diego, the war separated them for three more painful years.

God, give us eyes to see other people in need all around us. Give us a heart that yields to the sight, hands that touch, and minds that think so that we might serve one another with our gifts like

Barnabas did. Someone needs us to use our gift—it was given to us for a reason. God uses our hands and feet to bless others, if we are willing to let Him.

Nothing makes us feel more alive than lending our strength to another. Seek God every day and He will use you in a powerful way. Living out your calling is exciting and fulfilling. As you seek God, examine your gifts and pray about how you can use them for His glory. Try to grow and improve your skills. Embrace your calling. Someone needs your gifts. Like Barnabas, use all you have been given! This draws you nearer to God's heart.

1. Write out three Scriptures about encouraging others and discuss them with a group. Write a prayer asking God to show you specific ways you can encourage others, and then do it.

2. What do you love to do? What things come naturally to you? What can't you *not* do? Make a list of as many of your gifts, talents, and personal resources as you can think of.

3. Ask people who know you what gifts and talents they see in you. Write down any new insights you receive. Discuss with a group how your gifts could be used to serve God.

4. Examine all that God has given to you. Can you detect a pattern or connection between your gifts? Can they be combined to enable a purpose or ministry? Try writing down your calling and sharing it with someone. If you're not sure yet, pray regularly for God to reveal it to you.

5. Paul wrote: "In his grace, God has given us different gifts for doing certain things well. So if God has given you the ability to prophesy, speak out with as much faith as God has given you. If your gift is serving others, serve them well. If you are a teacher, teach well. If your gift is to encourage others, be encouraging. If it is giving, give generously. If God has given you leadership ability, take the responsibility seriously. And if you have a gift for showing kindness to others, do it gladly," (Rom. 12:6-8, NLT).

According to Paul, how are we to exercise our gifts? Name some ways you are currently using your gifts to glorify God and to serve others. How does using your gifts make you feel?

6. Discuss the stories of Derek Redmond and my grandmother. How did people come alongside of them in their time of need? What talents and resources did they use? Brainstorm with a group or journal about how you could come alongside other people and meet their needs.

CHAPTER 12

When Seeking Ends

Seeing God Face to Face

*Then we will no longer be immature like children. We won't be
tossed and blown about by every wind of new teaching. We will
not be influenced when people try to trick us with lies so clever
they sound like the truth. Instead, we will speak the truth in love,
growing in every way more and more like Christ, who is the head
of his body, the church.*

EPHESIANS 4:14-15 NLT

"Any day at the beach is a good day," I said to myself with a
smile. And what a beautiful day it was. Mike had to work, so
I had taken the kids by myself for a few days to Perdido Key,
Florida, right before school started. While we had a lot of fun, I
have to admit that the trip was a bit draining.

Being with teenagers sometimes requires *abundant* patience.
Since we were on vacation, they wanted to sleep all day and
watch movies all night. They could hardly carry on a coherent
conversation because they were constantly distracted with texts
and YouTube. They left an icky trail of wet towels, flip-flops,

and dirty dishes behind them. After all, they were on holiday, right? One wanted to fish, while another wanted to go shopping. I ended up serving as the referee, maid, and trip manager. Even though my kids were in high school, I challenged, consoled, shared, and even enforced some ground rules.

That vacation is a great example of the parenting experience. Sometimes it's so fun, and yet, when you're a parent, you're never off the job. You're always on duty, serving as a caretaker, a counselor, or even a cop. There is always a part of you that must be responsible and caring. Even when my kids are away, I sometimes wake up in the middle of the night, concerned for their well-being. I often crawl up on my knees and pray right there in the bed—sometimes with tears. It's vital to prepare and shape our children for life while we can. It's a heavy responsibility, an odd mix of duty and joy.

One day during that week of vacation, while the kids threw the football on the beach, I took a few moments to stroll across the white sand as the setting sun slowly nestled between orange, persimmon, and lavender clouds. The cool water lapped over my feet and the wind in my face felt wonderfully peaceful. As I walked along the shore, my mixed on-duty-parent feelings came into sharp focus, forming a visual picture of God and me.

This is what my relationship with Him is like.

I realized that God must feel the same way I do. As my heavenly parent, He is always on the job: counseling, teaching, challenging, and shaping. For as long as I live, He keeps working with me. He allows room for me to make mistakes and to fail. He has to be really patient, willing to work around my weakness and the messes I make. He pushes me to grow and mature.

While God takes great delight in me, like I do in my kids, the relationship has limitations. God and I are not just "free to be."

He has to enforce some rules, make some unpopular decisions, and be the heavy at times. The relational dynamic is teacher-student, immortal-mortal, potter-clay, and Father-child.

But while this is what our relationship with Him is like now, it won't always be this way. Someday, our journey of seeking will be over. Faith will be replaced with sight. Questions will be replaced with knowledge. We will see God face to face in all His wonder. There will be no more listening in silence or straining for glimpses of glory. We will graduate from the school of seeking with a degree in spiritual maturity. We will dance weightlessly in the sunset with God, like the clouds and light danced as I walked toward them along the seashore.

But not yet. Now is our time to seek. The time God set apart for learning, walking, and growing is our finite time here on Earth. One day, we won't need shaping anymore. We won't have to struggle against our flesh. Our weapons and spiritual armor will be put away. Pain will cease. School will be over; the lessons will be learned. Our problems and weaknesses will be discarded like old shells along the beach. We will emerge as entirely new creatures, complete and perfect.

When that happens, the dynamic of our relationship with God will change forever. Not that we will be equal, but His job will be done. We'll be home safely because He led us there each step of the way. No doubt, there will be more things to learn and discover, but the lessons will be fun; no pruning, heartache, or suffering will be needed. The tug-of-war between love and discipline will not be a part of our experience. Our fellowship with God will have no barriers. Our role will be royal instead of remedial. Our relational dynamic with Him will be one of teacher-graduate, immortal-immortal, potter-pottery, previously glazed and fired in the kiln. But until we get to heaven, His job is not done.

How good God is to teach, encourage, shape, and mold us right now. He is tireless. He makes hard decisions for our good that are painful for both of us. God is always revealing Himself in bite-sized pieces so we can understand. He uses visual aids in His teaching, like sunsets and clouds, sand and shells, children and parenting. He guides us, helps us overcome, restores and renews.

When all that stops, what will it be like? How will it feel? We'll never say the wrong thing or have to apologize. We won't be selfish or thoughtless anymore. Our relationship with God won't take any work or striving or seeking; it will soar, effortlessly like the wind. I can't even dream of it. My mind is too small and God's promises are too big. Eternity with God will be unlike anything we've ever known before. Our language has no words to describe it.

I can't wait. I hope to join you there. I am thankful that you joined me here, and walked with me along the way, seeking God through this book. There is a time for all things. For now, our (life) time is to be used for seeking God with all of our hearts; to go after Him like the saints and sinners before us. They can teach us things we may have never discovered on our own. They went deep—deep enough to change, serve, and impact lives. They went from glory to glory, and so can we, by seeking His familiar face.

Seek and Find

1. How is God working to mature you right now? What encouragement, discipline, or teaching has He given you?

2. Which biblical character in this book was the most helpful example of seeking God to you? Why?

3. What is your favorite example or story from this book? Why?

4. What have you learned in this book about seeking God that you didn't know before?

5. What is the main lesson you are taking away with you? Spend some time journaling about and discussing what you have learned. How might seeking God transform you from glory to glory (2 Cor. 3:18)?

Acknowledgements

When thank you seems so trite, I must say it anyway, for there are no better words to express my gratitude to the people who have blessed me so greatly.

I must start first by thanking the One who took hold of me, our glorious Lord (Father, Son, and Spirit). You took a negative—and honestly, sometimes bitter—person and changed me forever by Your grace. I can't help but write and talk about Your greatness because I have witnessed it in my own life. Glory, honor, and thanks to You.

To my dear husband, Mike, I thank you. You encouraged me to fly when I wanted to hide, you read my chapters (a lot) and prayed for me. Every. Single. Day. Thank you for generously letting me write about our experiences together and for not letting me quit. You are my best friend and the love of my life.

Thank you to my wonderful children, Will, Bryant, Caroline and my son-in-law, Jake. You have all helped me in many different ways. What a wonderful blessing you are!

Thank you to my wonderful encourager and friend, Andrea Wilhelm, who also happens to be my graphic artist and fellow collaborator on many projects. I can't wait to see what God will do with your vast store of talent. Thank you for using your gifts for God!

To Traci Mullins of Eclipse Editorial Services, my editor
extraordinaire who patiently taught me how to write cohesive
chapters, thank you! Your encouragement, insight and vast
experience were a Godsend. I am so grateful for your help in
getting this book to the finish line.

To Susan Tolleson of Propel Book Coaching, thank you for
helping me make this book better. Working at all hours of the
night is your specialty. You even prayed with me about this book
over the phone. You blessed my work in a special way!

To my sister, Lisa Yokley, thank you for going well beyond the
sister obligation in helping me edit this book.

To the wonderful people who have let me write about your
rich and colorful stories in this book, thank you so much! They
include: my family, Ty and Nancy Osman, Curtis and Devry
Coghlan, Art Leslie, Jesse May, Garrett Martz, Beth Bice,
Mitchell Brown, the family of Mary Ann Mercer, Beth Moshier,
Talitha Yokley, Carol May, Lauribeth White, Rica McRoy, and
Willena Steele.

To my writing critique group who read, prayed, encouraged and
advised—Write Out rocks! Thanks to Katie Taylor, Katie Wilson,
Toya Poplar, Kelly Mize, April Boddie, and Rashida Wilson.

To my prayerful biblical counseling friends, Willena Steele
and Maggie Merryman, thank you for encouraging me and for
listening—not many people do that. Your hearts are precious in
His sight and mine.

Thanks to my wonderful Fab 5 friends: Carol May, Beth Moshier, Talitha Yokley, and Karen Kimbrough. God has used you to grow and teach me for over twenty years! I love you and hope that I can be as much of a blessing to you as you have been to me.

To Denise George, my first writing teacher, thank you for introducing me to the world of writing! Your Writer's Boot Camp is awesome.

To my parents, Ray and Libby Jones, mother-in-law Carol Patterson, teachers, friends, church family and encouragers, thank you for being a part of my life.

To every single blog reader and subscriber: your encouragement means more to me than you will ever know. Thank you for every time you read, commented, shared a post or invited one more to join us. I love our special community of faith at maypatterson.com.

Notes

CHAPTER 1: SEEKING A FAMILIAR FACE

[1] A.W. Tozer, *The Pursuit of God*, (Camp Hill, PA: Christian Publications, 1982), 34.

[2] Mark Batterson, *The Circle Maker*, (Grand Rapids, MI: Zondervan, 2011), 157.

CHAPTER 2: JOSIAH

[1] Mrs. C.H. Morris, "Nearer, Still Nearer," 1898, Public Domain.

CHAPTER 3: MOSES

[1] The Glory of God, © 2014 by May Patterson

CHAPTER 4: THE THIEF

[1] Anne Lamott, *Bird by Bird*, (New York: Anchor Books, 1995), 121.

CHAPTER 5: MARY OF BETHANY

[1] Interview with Nancy Osman on May 1, 2017. For further information about Ty Osman's life and his memorial foundation, go to ty2foundation.org

CHAPTER 6: ZACCHAEUS

[1] Everett Ferguson, *The Early Church at Work and Worship*, Volume 1, (Eugene, OR: Cascade Books, 2013), 85.

[2] John Skinner, *The Confession of Saint Patrick*, (New York: Doubleday, 1998), 1.

CHAPTER 7: DAVID

[1]Mark Batterson, *The Circle Maker*, (Grand Rapids, MI: Zondervan, 2011), 152.

CHAPTER 8: ELIJAH

[1] Ibid

CHAPTER 9: RUTH

[1] Conversation with author, Kevin Elko, on August 3, 2016.

CHAPTER 10: HANNAH

[1] Conversation with Curtis and Devry Coghlan, missionaries, on December 8, 2016.

[2] For further information on the Coghlans and Kenya Relief, go to kenyarelief.org

[3] Surrender Is, © 2017 by May Patterson

CHAPTER 11: BARNABAS

[1] Bos, Carole, "Derek Redmond—The Day that Changed My Life," AwesomeStories.com. Jan 31, 2016. Accessed on Aug 11, 2017.

[2] For further information on Outback America, go to outbackamerica.org.

[3] For further information on the Huntsville Inner City Learning Center, go to: http://hiclc.org

[4] Ray Jones, *Citizen Soldier: Carl T. Jones*, (Huntsville, AL: 2016), 95.

About the Author

May Patterson, author of the book *Seeking a Familiar Face*, began writing in response to God's grace. And by His grace, she has written the Bible study *A Time to Seek*, articles for magazines such as *Focus on the Family* and *Upper Room*, and is a sought-after public speaker. She loves to tell stories, laugh, and talk about the incredible journey of seeking after God.

May feels blessed to have lived in Huntsville, Alabama all of her life. She is married to her dear friend Mike and they have three grown children. When she is not writing or speaking, you might find her on a hiking trail, riding a horse, or even aboard an airplane traveling to somewhere new. She has a great love for family, outdoor adventures, books and blogging at maypatterson.com.